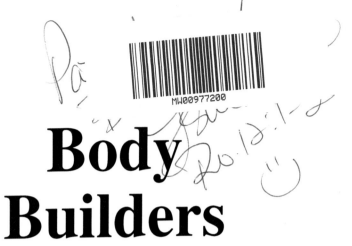

Body Builders

"CROSS" TRAINING

Building the Church Body through
Spiritual, Emotional, Mental &
Physical Fitness

Romans 14:12
"So then, each of us will give an account
of himself to God"

By Leslie Nease, AFC

xulon
PRESS

TABLE OF CONTENTS

PART THREE: ETERNAL FITNESS

DEDICATION

To my husband, Rod, your faithfulness and prayers are so important to me. Thank you for believing in me, supporting me and accepting me, quirks and all! God blessed my socks off when He sent you to me. I love you more each day.

****

To my precious children, Stephanie, Tommy, Kennedy and Peyton, thank you so much for your hugs, kisses and unconditional love. I am so blessed to share my life with such beautiful people – inside and out! I love you all.

****

To my mentor, Linda, your guidance, truthfulness and friendship is such a blessing. I know time is valuable, and I am grateful you spend so much of yours with me.

****

Most importantly – thank you Lord Jesus Christ for giving me purpose, vision and passion to further your Kingdom.

PREFACE

While attending a spiritual gifts assessment class at my church, I learned that my highest ranking spiritual gift from God is encouragement. I guess I already knew that was a top priority for me, but it was fun taking the little test and getting some confirmation.

I also took a passion analysis to really focus in on where my heart lies in ministry. I always thought ministry meant something already established in the church, like leading a Bible Study, the Women's or Men's Ministry, Youth, Preschool, or something like that. I never realized that God can take a passion you might have that is not necessarily a ministry within the walls of a church building, like fitness, and use it for His purpose in and out of the church. Ministry follows Christians, Christians don't necessarily have to follow ministry. It's important that we, as Christians, realize this truth. We are all in the ministry, whether we realize it or not. **Your life *is a ministry*.**

As I prayed and sought God's plan for my life each day, I started realizing more and more that He wants me to help teach others how important spiritual, emotional, mental *and* physical fitness are, especially for His children. I decided to start saturating myself with scripture until I could see where

God wanted me to go with this ministry.

As I did this, a strong feeling came over me. I really felt that God was not only saddened by the sedentary state of Americans, but I feel strongly that He is also righteously angry with us for letting ourselves get this way. There are so many strong warnings in the Bible about idols, sin and disobedience to God! When we become slaves to food, it is our idol, when we are gluttons, we are sinning and when we mistreat God's temple, it is disobedience. Paul says in 1 Corinthians 4:2 *"Now it is <u>required</u> that those who have been given a trust must prove faithful"*. God has given us these temporary bodies as a trust. He does not believe we are proving faithful in the way we are treating them.

As I prayed and asked the Lord to show me scripture to share with you, I was amazed how many scriptures He revealed to me that are very strong-worded and extremely convicting. In 1 Corinthians 3:17 it clearly states that *"If anyone destroys God's temple, <u>God will destroy him</u>; for God's temple is sacred, and you are that temple"*.

God showed me that Body Builders was to combine encouragement with a hefty dose of the fear of God. Three days before publication deadline, I was reading my morning devotion and it talked about the potter's clay and referred to Jeremiah 18. I then went on-line to read another devotion by another writer and it referred to the exact same passage. So I decided to see what it had to say.

I opened it up and read something that was extremely timely and very relevant to what the message the Lord wants to send out about the sin of gluttony. This passage says (Jeremiah 18:11b) *"This is what the Lord says: Look! I am preparing a disaster for you and devising a plan against you. So turn from your evil ways, each one of you, and reform your ways and your actions. But they will reply 'It's no use. We will continue with our own plans; each of us will follow the stubbornness of his evil heart.'"* It then goes on to say in verses 15-16 *"Yet my people have forgotten me; they burn incense to worthless idols, which made them stumble in their ways and in the ancient paths. They made them walk in bypaths and on roads not built up. Their land will be laid waste; an object of lasting scorn; all who pass by will be appalled and will shake their heads".*

I underlined that last part because it really reminded me of America today. I was talking to a missionary the other day who pointed out that they had been overseas for a few years and when they came back, they could not believe how *big* Americans were. People in other countries look at us like we are a bunch of gluttons who live in excess, and I fear God views us that way, too. It's time to wake up and be the warriors God created us to be! It's time to fight.

He wants me, of all people, to help get the word out to people that we need to change. I knew in order to do this, I would be using scripture that may make some people feel uncomfortable, or make them feel conviction from the Holy Spirit. I wasn't sure I wanted to do this. My whole life has been spent as an encourager, someone who likes making people happy and helping them feel good about themselves.

As I continued to seek His plan for my life, I prayed, asking God for guidance. I asked Him why He would even consider using me, an encourager, to deliver a message of correction. I didn't feel qualified and I certainly didn't feel it was "in my comfort zone". I felt a sense of peace as God showed me that having a gift of encouragement might actually have its benefits in delivering the message God wants me to deliver.

I would want an encourager to deliver a message of correction to me, wouldn't I? Someone who could point me to the truth and then afterward, they would come along side of me with encouragement and exhortation. I decided to start putting some of the scriptures I had found together and some of my life experiences to make a seminar to help people understand the importance of combining spiritual, mental and physical fitness. I felt I should call it "Body Builders" – as in building up the *church* body.

As I started putting more and more together, I wanted to write down, word for word, what I would want to say in this seminar and have someone who is rooted in sound doctrine, a pastor or teacher, to look it over and "proof" it for me. As I started to do this, the words just kept coming. Body Builders was turning into a book – much to my surprise! I have written a fitness column for a couple of years, but never had I tried my hand at a book, nor did I think I was qualified to do something like that. But God is not interested in the limits I put on myself. *He is more interested in the unlimited potential of His children when they are allowing Him to lead them.*

You will not find all the answers to your problems in this book. I'm not a perfect, all together, Proverbs 31 woman or even close to that, but I am a woman after God's heart and I know He's got the answers I was so desperately looking for. You will see I've had a lot of the same struggles you may have had in life, but I cannot take credit for the transformation in my life that has taken place.

You see, a relationship with Jesus Christ is the most transforming thing there is in the world. If you want to build a body that glorifies God, remember He must be invited into your life in order to change it from the *inside, out.* You must surrender control to God and give Him complete authority over your life. Trust me - He can do a *much* better job than you can, even on a good day!

I wrote this book to encourage and help disciple Christians who have decided to follow the Lord Jesus Christ to the best of their ability. However, I realize that there may be people who read this book who have not yet made a decision to follow Christ. Maybe you are just searching for answers? If you are not sure you would go to heaven if you died today, I strongly encourage you to read the appendix in this book entitled "Eternal Fitness" which will show you how you can know beyond a shadow of a doubt that you will spend eternity with God in heaven. It's the most important decision you will ever make in your life.

The pages that follow are a result of conviction I've felt, experiences God has given me, scripture references I've been shown and the leading of the Holy Spirit. I hope you enjoy the journey as much as I have and may God bless you as you strive to build your body from the inside, out for God's purposes!

CHAPTER ONE:

OUT OF THE DARKNESS & INTO THE LIGHT (MY STORY)

Like so many children these days, I was a child of divorce. My mother, whom I dearly love and who did her best with me, had a lot of problems in her upbringing and had a difficult time finding happiness. She and my father divorced when I was 6 months old. She married my step-father when I was a toddler and he helped her raise my sister and I for a few years before their eventual divorce.

My step-father was an alcoholic in earlier days and he was gone a lot as a result of being deployed in the military. My mother was lonely, frustrated and felt her only choice was to move on. For a few years, we lived in a trailer park with our mother until she met another man who she married for just a couple of months. He was not very fond of us, nor were we of him. Mom seemed to always have our best interests in mind, so she left him in order to keep us from being unhappy.

She re-married my step-father a couple of years later when they both accepted Christ as their Savior. That was about the time that my "God Radar" starting going off. I even said a prayer once asking Jesus into my heart, but did not really understand what that meant – except that it meant I wouldn't go to hell. I was in fourth grade and had not been raised in a Christian home, so my level of spiritual understanding was pretty low. I see, in retrospect, that my quest for a relationship with God had just begun in those early years.

My family life changed a lot. It was a difficult road for my step-dad, because he had given up alcohol, committed his life to the Lord and was trying desperately to be a good Christian man. I respected him tremendously for that. He had a very obvious transformation at that point.

I was never able to develop a healthy relationship with my biological father much because we traveled around a lot due to my step-father being in the military and he lived in West Virginia. I love that I was able to travel, but found it difficult to build relationships because as soon as I'd make a friend, it would be time to move on. My sister and I became very close, though, and she and I were best friends growing up.

We moved to California in the early 1980's and went to a church where legalism was prevalent. My step-father became very involved in the children's bus ministry, where my sister and I would help him invite neighborhood children to church and give out candy every week. He eventually became very legalistic and controlling as a result of the church's influence. I do not blame him, nor do I think ill of him for this – I think discipleship is the most important thing that can happen once you become a Christian and unfortunately, we were in a church that did not lovingly show us how to develop a relationship with Christ, it only told us how we should live.

Works were all that mattered in our home. Our lives revolved around making sure nobody in the church saw us living in "sin". We were not allowed to wear pants, our television was taken out of our house, we had bon-fires where we burned all of our secular music, and we were absolutely terrified of the pastor in the church. I was in the 5th grade at this time, and I just remember trembling when he would come around because he was so terrifying. I started to be afraid of my step-father, too.

I asked for a pair of jeans for my birthday when I turned 12. My step-father said I could have a pair of 501 Levis (all the rage in those days) but that I was not to wear them out of the house under any circumstances. I agreed to those conditions because I was so excited about the fact that I would be able to just wear them at all!

One night, I put them in my big purse when I was going to the roller rink in my culottes (a skirt with a split up the center that I had to wear in lieu of pants) and I remember feeling like Cinderella at the ball when I changed into them at the roller rink bathroom. Everyone was impressed – they had never seen me in jeans. I loved the attention and I felt like a million bucks.

When I knew they were about to come pick me up, I changed back into the culottes and stuffed the jeans back in my purse. My mom picked me up and when we returned home, I was confronted by my parents. They had checked my drawers to see if I had taken the jeans to the roller rink. They insisted on seeing inside of my purse. When they found the jeans, I was put on restriction for 2 weeks.

I will never forget the feeling that I had at that moment. I hated God, I hated Christians, *I felt that Christianity was so rule focused that I'd never be able to live up to it.* I started thinking I wasn't really a Christian, or I wouldn't have wanted to wear jeans. I doubted my salvation and I was living in total fear. There was no relationship with God, just rules and an inability to follow those rules consistently. I felt overwhelming hopelessness.

We eventually left the legalistic church, but started receiving threatening mail from anonymous congregation members. We lost our best friends in the church because the Pastor told them that they could not "be unequally yolked" with us since we left the church. It was by far one of the worst experiences of my life and I still cringe when I think about the lack of love, broken relationships and extreme judgment we experienced there.

As a teen, I found my identity in popularity. I lived to feel accepted. We had moved to Okinawa, Japan right before my freshman year in high school, where I became a cheerleader and based my existence on making others happy. I didn't matter, only others did. I wanted everyone to like me. I wanted to feel loved and accepted for who I was, so I did everything possible to make myself worthy of others' acceptance, even compromising my values and morals.

My parents kept us going to church throughout high school. I hated going – it seemed we were there Sunday morning, Sunday night, Wednesday night prayer meeting, or whenever else the doors would open. The youth group basically consisted of my sister, me and a couple of other teens. There was another church on the island that had a huge, thriving youth group but my parents would not allow us to go to that one. They felt an allegiance to the church we were at because they were happy there, but my sister and I felt totally disconnected. We eventually became rebellious.

In 1986, I went away to college and I swore I'd have nothing to do with church, with God or with anything that had to do with it. I was living in total disillusionment and I felt lost.

I had a pretty bad reputation on campus as a result of some horrific decisions I made during this time. I was drinking, partying and making wrong choices with men. I look back at this time in my life and realize that I was looking to fill that void again – the void that God could only fill. I desperately wanted to be loved, and I thought guys would love me if I would give myself to them, I thought I'd be accepted if I drank and partied and I liked the "numb" feeling I got when I drank. It helped me to feel more confident and social when I drank, but the next morning I would always feel disgusted with myself.

My biological father lived near my college, but we still had a difficult time developing a healthy relationship. A lot of this had to do with my rebellion and I think that down deep I resented the fact that he was my father and I didn't even know him. He lived just 20 minutes away from my college, but the 2 years I spent there, we maybe saw each other a handful of times. When I would see him, I remember feeling overwhelmed and happy, but unable to show my feelings for fear of rejection. I just wanted to be loved so desperately. I was so ashamed of who I had become, though, that I felt like even if he did get to know me, he could never love me anyway.

I met my husband, Rod, during the summer of 1988 and he was living a hard life, too. I was drawn to him because he was the only guy I had ever met who really seemed to like me for who I was as a person, not for what I could give him. He and I started out as friends and quickly realized we were made for each other.

During this time, my mother and step father were going through a bitter divorce. This just proved my theory that Christianity was bogus, I thought. They could hardly stand to be around each other and I felt my empty feeling increase even more because I felt like "home" was stripped away from me again. I promised I would never get a divorce once I was married, I didn't want my children feeling this emptiness.

Rod and I ended up marrying in 1989 and had 2 children within 3 years. I had gained a lot of weight during both of my pregnancies and after the birth of my son in 1992, I was busting out of a size 16, weighing 185 pounds in a 5' 4" frame. I sank into a deep depression during this time. I felt like I was living in someone else's body, like I was a stranger to myself. I thought I was overweight because I had some sort of medical problem, so I started spending a lot of time at the doctor's office.

I think my doctor must have cringed when I would walk through the door each week. I couldn't understand my weight gain, I felt depressed and I needed something or someone to blame besides myself. I would spend hours crying about my weight and then I'd drink myself into oblivion every night to numb the pain.

My husband, who had always been so supportive, finally couldn't take it anymore. He said "Leslie, I love you no matter what you look like or how much you weigh but I can't stand to see you like this. You need to stop crying about it and get up and do something about it or I don't know how much longer I can stay married to you".

What a wake up call! He bought me a pair of running shoes and a membership to the local gym the next day. I realized, finally, that in order to be a healthy weight again, I had to get some exercise and change my lifestyle.

I'll never forget my first step class. I thought I would DIE! It was so hard – and I was really uncoordinated. I remember feeling totally defeated and exhausted just after the WARM UP! It seemed daunting, but the task had to be done.

My body responded very well to the exercise. Eventually, I even started teaching the classes myself. This kept me accountable, something I really needed to have in my life. I kept losing weight and everyone was noticing my weight loss. I was starting to feel accepted again. I started finding my identity in how I looked again, which was nice for me since when I was overweight, I had no identity (or so I thought).

After a couple of years, I had reached my goal weight of 125. I kept losing because the more I lost, the better I'd feel. I was in *control* and it felt great. I was now down to a size 4 and I was starting to look ill. People commented on how thin I was – my step mother even cried when she saw me. I remember thinking how ridiculous I thought that was. I was so twisted in my head.

I had what is described as "exercise bulimia". It's when you eat, but instead of purging the food, you exercise to get rid of the extra calories. This is an eating disorder that frequently gets overlooked in America. I was slowly wasting away.

A trainer at the gym asked me what was going on and showed me how to use weights to build muscle and gave me nutritional advice to help me put some weight on. I thank God for this person! I finally put some weight on, changed my eating habits and started focusing more on moderation.

My husband and I were starting to think more about God at this point. Our two children were getting to the age where they needed to be in church. It mattered to me that they were in church – but I can't explain why. I always promised myself I'd never make them go to church because I had so many bad experiences there. In retrospect, I can clearly see that God had never given up on me, not at all! Feeling convicted about going to church after having such a negative experience can only be explained as the work of God in my life – Him pursuing me and knowing I would eventually respond.

I became pregnant in 1998 and gave birth to our 3rd child in October. During my pregnancy, Rod and I had found a church and were really starting to be more "religious" because we thought that was best for our kids. We eventually had our last child in 2000 and after she was born, we were still going through the motions of church and Bible study.

Six months after the birth of our last child, I was still looking to fill a void in my life. I had competed in pageants before and found they were a great goal to put before myself in order to train and prepare my body. I began training to compete for the title of Mrs. North Carolina in 2001. I knew

I had some "baby" weight to lose and I thought this would help me to get motivated to get those extra pounds off. I had never actually won a pageant, but had been in several and I really enjoyed the competition and excitement of it all.

I ended up winning the title, much to my surprise and I thought that with that title the fulfillment I was so desperately searching for would certainly come. I spent the next year traveling around North Carolina educating people about the importance of physical fitness (my "platform"), signing autographs, participating in parades and making televised appearances.

I was honored to compete in the Mrs. United States Pageant in Las Vegas in August of 2001. It was very thrilling and a completely new experience for me. I did not win the national title, but walked away feeling like a winner because I had made it so far. Plus, I was making a difference in my community and that really made me feel good.

Unfortunately, being Mrs. North Carolina didn't take away that emptiness I had inside. What was it going to take to get my life on track? I started searching scriptures and going to more Bible studies at this point, trying to find truth.

I felt a strong urgency to pray for my husband's role as a spiritual leader of our home. He never prayed out loud, never initiated any Bible study and I felt like our lives were not reflecting the Lord at all. We were still drinking and partying on the weekends and I could feel myself slipping back into that numbness of alcoholism. My husband and I both drank a lot and we were co-dependent with it. I felt if he was drinking, it was okay for me and I think he felt the same way.

Alcohol was on my mind constantly. Instead of focusing on Christ, I was focused on my sin. I didn't feel like I could ever live without it. When I was drinking, that was the only time I truly felt like things were going to be okay in my life. But when I would wake, sober, the next day, I felt like I was living a double life – and I felt consumed with conviction. It was an overwhelming feeling to say the least.

Occasionally, I found myself in deep prayer with tears streaming down my face praying God would help us. I prayed for over 2 years for my husband to be the spiritual leader of our family, because I knew that I needed the accountability of having my husband walk beside me in Christ.

God led us to a wonderful church in Charlotte where they were offering a Discipleship class for new members. We decided to attend this weekend event. This was in February of 2003. The first night of the class, the pastor talked about Jesus and about the Holy Spirit in a way we had never heard before. He talked about surrendering. In a loving and understanding way, he explained how when we claim to be a Christian, we must live accordingly. He said if God was going to be able to provide abundant life to us, we must live daily in Him.

Then he asked the question "If you were to die right now, are you 100% sure you'd go to heaven?" My husband did not know the answer to this question. I can't even say for sure that I did. I knew I believed in Christ, but I questioned my decision to follow Him all the time because I continued to live and be controlled by sin. Obedience follows true surrender, and I was not being obedient at all.

My husband stood to his feet and acknowledged to everyone in the room that he wanted Jesus Christ as His Savior. I sat quietly in my seat, still wondering if I was saved or not, still unknowing. When the pastor said the prayer of salvation and asked us to repeat it from the *heart* I quietly said the prayer that I had said so many times before, but this time it was different. I was truly repentant. I was truly sorry for my sin and I did not want to live in sin anymore. The difference this time was that I wasn't just sorry, I'd had *enough!*

We were baptized a couple of weeks later, and I remember vividly as I was going down into the water, making my public profession of faith, that God was urging me to leave the alcohol in the water. When I immerged from the water, a warm feeling came over my entire body and I had a quick visual flash of me coming up into a new life – the alcohol had stayed in the water behind me. I knew this didn't mean I was going to be perfect, but I took it to mean that God definitely wanted me to turn from alcohol so I could focus more on a relationship with Him.

My husband and I had invited all of our friends to the baptism, some knew Christ, others were searching and others just thought we had gone completely insane but they loved us anyway, so they came! A week later, we were invited to a party where there was alcohol. Some of the friends who we had invited to witness our baptism were there. Yet again, we succumbed to temptation and ended up drinking at this party. However, the next day the Holy Spirit was working overtime in both of our lives. Our desire to change and repent was different.

We felt uneasy all that morning and finally that afternoon, we approached each other at the same time and said "NO MORE". We were both overwhelmed with conviction and felt that if we were going to be a testimony to our friends who did not know Christ, if we were going to continue to grow as Christians, we had to fully surrender everything, completely and totally, to Christ. For the first time ever, we really felt that we had the power to overcome the stronghold of alcohol in our lives. We have not had a drop of alcohol since, and I can honestly say I have no desire to. My desire is now for Christ. My desire is to fully dedicate my life to sharing the gospel with others.

Mind you, this is a daily surrender. Christ specifically says in Luke 9:23 *"If anyone would come after me, he must deny himself and take up his cross daily and follow me. For whoever wants to save his own life will lose it, but whoever loses his life for me will save it"*.

In order to stay surrendered, I've had to turn down several invitations to parties and some friends think I've completely cut off ties with them, but I know what I'm doing is necessary if I'm going to remain in Him. I don't want to lose any friends, but I know *I must also surround myself with Christian friends who know what I'm going through* and who support my new life because they are living the same surrendered existence. This helps keep my life in alignment.

I belong to a "Bunco" group (a group of women who get together once a month and play Bunco) in my neighborhood with 15 other women and I used to drink with them every month. I knew my life change would be obvious to them, so I felt led to share with them the reason for my change. I was due to have Bunco at my home this past summer and I knew they would expect to have alcohol there. I had promised God we would no longer have alcohol in our home, so I knew something had to be done. I wrote them a letter, explaining my life change and sharing my testimony with them. Here is the letter I gave to each of them:

To My Bunco Babe Buddies,

First, you guys ROCK! I'm having such a blast being a part of such wonderful women in our Bunco group. I've been with the group for almost 5 years now and I've seen a lot of people come and go along the way. It's such a great way to keep in touch with all of you during our busy lives – to know that I will see you guys at least once a month is awesome. So, thank you for being my friends and thank you for your unending support in all of my "quests" to get on tv, my spiritual journey, my pregnancies and all the other things in my life that have meant so much.

I just looked over this letter so far and realized that it sounds like I'm dying or something and that I'm saying goodbye!! No, that's not the case (well, not really). You see, I have died in a way. A lot of you know I've committed my life to the Lord and as a result, the old Leslie is pretty much dead and gone (it's a good thing – trust me!) I just wanted to share what's gone on in my life with you so you'd understand where I'm at and why I've changed so many things about my life.

Back on November 15, 1979, I heard the good news of the gospel and realized my need for a savior. I made a head decision to accept the free gift of eternal life by believing in Jesus Christ as my Savior, but (I'm going to use an analogy here!) it was like God gave me this beautifully wrapped gift with the most gorgeous, shiny paper and a lovely, colorful bow and I let the gift sit on my table for 24 years UNOPENED. Oh, I told people about my gift – I even peeked inside every now and then. But until February of this year, I had not opened it to accept what was inside of it.

Let me explain what all of this means before I completely lose you here! You see, in order to fully appreciate what it is that salvation truly is, you must "open" the gift. In order to do this, you must surrender you life completely to Jesus Christ. He has a purpose for your life – a very important one – and until you surrender control to Him and only Him, you cannot fulfill that purpose. You must die to yourself and then He can live through you. Your passions will then change and you will be able to walk hand in hand with the creator of the Universe who will guide you daily.

My "head" decision to accept the Lord back in 1979 was good spiritual step in the right direction, but my recent "heart" decision to fully surrender my life to the Lord has sealed my salvation and completely changed me.

Rod and I realized that as we searched for what was missing in our lives, we were in a lot of pain (emotionally) since we were not living in God's Will. As a result, we turned to alcohol. Many of you would be shocked to know how much I really was drinking. I was truly an alcoholic and this realization was extremely painful and embarrassing.

No, I didn't drink the minute I woke up but it was something I didn't feel I could live without. That was the first thing the Lord revealed to me that had to go. So, I'm proud and excited to say that we haven't had a drop of alcohol in 4 months! (All thanks to God – we couldn't have done it without him). That's why I'm not serving alcohol tonight at our Bunco party. Let me make this very clear – I in no way think that alcohol is bad or something God wouldn't want anyone to do in order to be a Christian! I just felt like it was not something he wanted ME to do. So please, do not feel like I'm judging any of you or anyone else for that matter! If it was something I could control, I wouldn't have a problem having a few drinks every now and then.

Anyway, I just wanted to share this news with you because you mean SO much to me and I know you probably have a lot of questions about what's going on with me. I want to say one last thing to you before I close this letter because I feel like it's my responsibility to ask: Have you entered into a personal relationship with Jesus Christ? Do you know without a doubt, 100% that you'd go to heaven if you died right now? I have so much I can share with you about this if you don't have the answers to these two questions.

You know I'm a sane, happy, normal person with good reasoning skills and I'm not a crazy crackpot – so you know this decision I've made comes with merit. Is this a decision you need to make for you and your future? If so, please let me know if you need more information or if you want to talk one on one about anything. Nothing would make me happier than to share my faith with you. If you already have a personal relationship with Jesus, I thank God so much that I will be able to play Bunco with you into all eternity!

No matter how you react to this letter, please know I love you, you're awesome and I'm forever grateful that you've taken the time to read what the Lord has asked me to share with you! God bless you and keep you until our next Bunco Babe Bash!

In His Love,
Leslie

The love and appreciation I received from these women completely touched me. They all understood, were very supportive and some even sent me thank you cards in the mail. I know it helps me to be accountable by coming into the light (so to speak) and just telling everyone the truth about myself. Now I've stepped out of the darkness and into the light publicly and when they have questions about God or Jesus, they know they have someone they can trust and ask. I am so humbled that God used me in this way. He delights in using us in such ways!

In retrospect, I realize that being brought up in the church, whether legalistic or not, was better than not having its influence at all. I see now that God's word was still penetrating my soul – Hebrews 4:12 says *"For the word of God is living and active. Sharper than any double-edged sword, it penetrates even to dividing soul and spirit, joints and marrow; it judges the thoughts and attitudes of the heart".*

The word of God cannot be heard and not felt. It made an impression on me – and even though we were in a legalistic atmosphere, I thank God that my family brought us up in the church. God is so good!

God really blessed me with a strong Christian mother-in-law, who I believe has been on her knees for us since the day we were married. She is wise and strong and I am grateful for having someone like this in my life that I can turn to for guidance and prayer. My biological father has also turned to Christ and completely surrendered himself. He and his sweet wife have been Christians for several years and I feel their prayers, as well.

My mother and step-father eventually found other spouses and they are all serving the Lord now. I have a tremendous amount of gratitude for my step father and my mother. They had so much to do with my being brought up in the Word of God and I know they've been praying for me all along. My step-dad is no longer living a life of legalism and I know he will continue to serve God faithfully the rest of his life. My mom and step dad taught me how to rise above situations and to keep Christ first in my life, regardless of the influences around us.

I've realized that, aside from my family, I have two very strong passions in my life. Those two passions are Christianity and fitness. It's funny how God works – those are the two things I've struggled most with in my life and now they are my passions! Sometimes I ask God why he instilled these two specific passions in me – *the two things that nobody seems to want to commit to because they take a great deal of personal sacrifice in time, patience, willpower and endurance.*

That's just my flesh crying out – asking God to take away this burden for spiritual and physical fitness in the church body. With God's help though, I press on because He gives me a peace knowing that I was created for a purpose and that purpose is to share the gospel and whatever other gifts he gives me to use to further His Kingdom.

I wanted to tell you my story so you could understand where I'm coming from. I've had a lot of personal struggles, struggles I feel were filled with purpose and certainly God has taken what Satan meant for harm and turned it around for His good.

I've spent a good portion of my life trying so hard to do better, to be a better person. I remember praying desperately to God and telling Him I would try harder next time. Then as I read the scriptures, I realized that it didn't matter how hard I tried in my own power, I could not get better. I needed to surrender my fears, my failures, my self-loathing, my lifestyle and my habits to Him and allow Him to do the work for me. Actually, He already did the work for me when He died on that cross for me. I just needed to come to that realization. Once I did, He completely changed my life. I feel like Christ is saying, as He did in John 16:31 *"You believe at last"!* My life will never again be the same – ***and I praise God for that!***

PART ONE:

COMPLETE FITNESS

CHAPTER TWO

GOD'S HOLY TEMPLE

"You are no longer foreigners and aliens, but fellow citizens with God's people and members of God's household, built on the foundation of the apostles and prophets, with Christ Jesus Himself as the Chief Cornerstone. In him the whole building is joined together and rises to become a holy temple in the Lord. And in him <u>you too are being built together to become a dwelling in which God lives by His Spirit</u>" Ephesians 2:19-22.

The disciples of Jesus were fearful and distressed right before He was to be put to death; they did not want him to go. They felt that they would not be able to learn the same truths they were learning when they walked beside Him and feared they would miss Him terribly. Jesus, always the Comforter, said to them *"I will ask the Father, and he will give you another Counselor to be with you forever – the Spirit of truth. The world cannot accept him, because it neither sees him nor knows him. But you know him, for he lives with you and will be in you."* –John 14:16-17

Here are some more scripture references that speak about the indwelling of the Holy Spirit in a child of God:

"What agreement is there between the temple of the living God and idols, as God has said "I will live with them and walk among them, and I will be their God and they will be my people" -2 Corinthians 6:16 (note from me – please don't get hung up on this word "idols" – we will discuss it later on in the book!)

> *"Do you not know that your body is the temple of the Holy Spirit, who is in you, whom you have received from God? You are not your own; you were bought at a price. Therefore honor God with your body".*
> 1 Corinthians 6:19-20

These scriptures really put things into perspective for Christians. My soul is deeply moved when I realize that **the God of the Universe dwells inside of me,** helping me to make the right choices, giving me wisdom and guidance as I search the scriptures and interceding for me to the Father when I don't know how to pray.

Christians should instinctively rejoice when they read reassurances like this in God's word, remembering that not only do they have a tremendous gift from God by having an indwelling of the Holy Spirit, but they also have tremendous *responsibility* in being a temple of the Holy Spirit.

When you think of a temple, what do you think of?

A temple is a sacred place of worship. Our lives should be a constant reminder of the fact that we are sacred – set aside for God's purpose, not our own. Webster defines sacred as "dedicated or set apart for the worship of a deity; devoted exclusively to one service or use; <u>entitled to reverence and respect</u>".

King Solomon built a temple for God and it took seven long years. He took great pride in building this temple, as it was a task that God had put before him. When I read this story in 1 Kings, chapter 6, I am awestruck with the great detail Solomon put into this temple. He had only the best cedar, pine and stone to build the temple and then he decorated it with bronze, gold, cherubim, carvings and beams.

Solomon treated this temple with the utmost respect. He did not take lightly that the God Almighty was going to be dwelling there and he made sure even the smallest detail was painstakingly carried out.

Once the temple was completed, Solomon fell on his knees with his arms outstretched and dedicated the temple to God. He asked God to make sure that all the people of the earth would know God's name and fear Him as a result of the temple bearing God's name (1 Kings 8:43).

We realize that in Old Testament times, this was important, because this is where God dwelled. People would approach the temple and pray, seek forgiveness, direction, repentance and teaching from God. We are now living in times where God actually dwells inside of *us* once we accept Jesus as our Savior. Since we know this to be true, we realize that our body is a temple. People of the earth should know God's name and fear Him as a result of our temples bearing God's name.

How are you treating God's temple?

Currently in America, 69% of our population is overweight. Of those, 35% (or maybe even more now) are actually in the obese category. Obese is 30 pounds over the ideal weight. Obesity is the second leading cause of preventable deaths in the US, second only to tobacco deaths. Last year, over 300,000 people died as a result of obesity-related illnesses while 400,000 people died due to tobacco-related illnesses.

According to the Center for Disease Control, since

1991, the obesity rate in America has risen 74%. In an age where you don't even have to get up to change the television channel, we have become a sedentary, lazy generation of gluttons. Gluttony sounds like a terrible word – I always imagined it was someone who was morbidly obese, stuffing food in their face with reckless abandon. However, the true definition of a glutton is "someone who drinks or eats in excess". I'd say most Americans fall into that category at some point in their lives.

There can be no doubt that Satan is using this disease to shorten our life span, effect the quality of our lives, hinder our ministry and give us lack of confidence. In America, obesity is such a delicate issue because the roots of the disease are so deep. Many people are turning to food for comfort, for pleasure, for companionship or out of boredom.

In the Gospel of John, John writes about a time when Jesus went up to Jerusalem. He found people in the temple courts that were selling animals and exchanging money as if the temple were a shopping mall.

You see, many people traveled back in those days, but they still had to offer sacrifices to God for repentance because Jesus had not yet been offered as the Ultimate Sacrifice for sin. In order to have sacrifices to offer at the temples, people who traveled would purchase an animal from a vendor in front of the temple since their animals were usually not with them.

Sacrifice is giving up something of worth to you that you have invested time and energy into and Jesus felt these people weren't really sacrificing at all – that they were going through the motions of sacrifice with these purchased substitutes. This made Jesus righteously angry (on a side note, between you and me, it's a comfort to hear that Jesus got righteously angry sometimes!). He was also angry that the people in the temple seemed to have lost sight of the reason it was built in the first place – to worship and pray to God.

In John 2:15-17 John describes the scene: *So he (Jesus) made a whip out of cords, and drove all from the temple area, both sheep and cattle; he scattered the coins of the money changers and overturned their tables. To those who sold doves, he said "Get these out of here! How dare you turn my Father's house into a market"! His disciples remembered that it is written: "**Zeal for your house will consume me**".*

I was in a Bible study a few months ago and the subject of this verse came up. We were all talking about what the scripture meant to us. As we were sharing, one gentleman said something that really stuck with me. He said he thought Jesus might be foretelling how he gets filled with righteous anger when people treat God's temple with disrespect – and we all know that *we are God's Temple* now.

This really spoke to my heart. I realized that not only does the Lord feel sadness when we treat ourselves with disrespect, but that He actually gets righteously angry – as well He should. *When we become Christians, we are not our own anymore.* We belong to Christ. We should be living lives that reflect God's presence in our lives.

We usually consider that putting things like illegal or unhealthy substances into our bodies or sexual immorality as sin. Did we ever take into consideration that the act of gluttony (clearly referred to as a sin in the Bible – Proverbs 23:21) and the act of laziness (also clearly a sin in the Bible – Hebrews 6:12) are also sin? If this offends or convicts you in any way, please understand that *you are the very person I am hoping will benefit from reading this book and applying the Biblical truths to your life.* Remember, I've been there.

God sees that we are not treating our bodies as His sacred temple. We are responsible for the upkeep of the body and the spirit. It is up to us to make healthy food choices, get enough sleep and exercise. I realize these bodies are temporary and that they have no eternal value, but the value they have on earth are to house the Holy God of the Universe – until the day Christ returns. Shouldn't we be making upkeep a priority?

On the other hand, I realize that there are some people who are obsessed with keeping their bodies in shape, but spiritually they are drying up, starving and thirsty. There is an alignment here that needs to be discussed so we can come to some common ground and live lives that reflect our faith. If we want to live lives that can really make a difference for God, we need to be energized, healthy and confident.

We do have hope though – blessed hope through Jesus Christ! He wants to help us overcome our strongholds, no matter what they may be. He actually already overcame them on the cross. Jesus was acquainted with grief and he knows what suffering feels like (see Isaiah 53) so you can be sure He knows how it feels to struggle. I encourage you to go through this book with hope in your heart and with a desire to get closer to Christ and embrace His mercy and love.

It's time for a change!

CHAPTER THREE

"FAT AND HAPPY" IN AMERICA

I've noticed a lot of people use the term "fat and happy" to describe themselves when they feel like they are doing well in America. This is another lie Satan is feeding us – that we need to live the life of excess in order to be happy.

The American Dream is something that people strive for – the house with the white picket fence, the 2.2 kids, 1 dog, perfect job and a life of self-indulgent excess. It's as if we feel we deserve it. We say we are the land of the free, but are we? It seems to me we are slave to keeping up with the "Joneses". That's not freedom – that's slavery.

Food is one of our masters in America. We enjoy it so much that we've super-sized our portions, made it more convenient, and we spend millions of dollars per year on foods that are advertised on the television and in magazines. *Some of us live to eat, when we should be eating to live.*

I remember not too long ago that a fast food restaurant came out with a commercial where they did an extreme close-up on a cheeseburger (trying to tempt us) and then the actor exclaimed how he had to have one *now* upon whence the announcer happily exclaims "We're open late!", as if to lure some unsuspecting person off the couch and into their car to go get the burger, no matter what time it was. We are bombarded with advertising like this every day.

Many of my "feel good" memories from childhood take me back to times in Grandma's kitchen, dinners around the table, the smell of Thanksgiving dinner, baking with mom, and church get-togethers with casseroles and food scattered all over the table. If I was having a bad day, mom would make my favorite dinner or make a batch of cookies to help cheer me up.

I am not saying that eating food is bad or that any of my childhood experiences were wrong – but what I am saying is that in some place in my mind, I've eventually come to a place where food is comfort for me. It's familiar, it envelopes my senses. It gives me a sense of belonging and it creates a wonderful atmosphere for fellowship.

When most church groups get together, the first question they throw around is "What are you going to bring to eat?" I searched the scriptures everywhere and found nothing anywhere that says "Where two or more are gathered in God's name, there is a casserole amongst them"! I once attended a church and tried to find a small group to fit into and all of the leaders were complaining about how difficult it is to organize who's bringing what. Some leaders were even dropping out because they were so frustrated! I am sure that this is not something God wants going on in His church family.

I understand that food is good and it is an important source of fellowship, but I think when we start taking the focus off of Jesus and putting it on who's bringing what, we're missing the point. Jesus said *"My food is to do the will of Him who sent me, and to finish His work" (John 4:34)*. Now that's keeping priorities straight.

It's obvious that in Biblical days, food was an important

source of fellowship, too. Jesus broke bread with many people, and communion was always done around a meal. However, there is a difference between the ancient days and today.

First, in those days, there was a lot more physical activity. They did not have cell phones, automobiles, televisions, computers, microwaves, dishwashers or even refrigerators. In order to make a meal, it was quite a process. In the Bible, there are many references to the effort it took to just prepare a meal:

> 1 Samuel 28:24-25: *The woman had a fattened calf at the house, which she butchered at once. She took some flour, kneaded it and baked bread without yeast. Then she set it before Saul and his men, and they ate. That same night they got up and left.*

> Luke 10:38-40: *As Jesus and his disciples were on their way, he came to a village where a woman named Martha opened her home to him. She had a sister called Mary, who sat at the Lord's feet listening to what he said. But Martha was distracted by all the preparations that had to be made. She came to him and asked, "Lord, don't you care that my sister has left me to do all the work by myself? Tell her to help me!".*

Martha must have had some serious work set before her. She actually commanded the Creator of the Universe to tell Mary to help her! She's got some nerve. Goodness, if she were in today's society, she could have ordered a pizza and sat down herself.

I know there are many more scripture references

concerning food preparation, but I think you get the point. The woman in 1 Samuel had to kill the calf, divide the meat and cook it over an open flame, make bread from scratch and then serve it to the gentlemen who, apparently, got up and left after the meal. That's a lot of energy spent for one meal. She probably "worked off" the calories from the meal just in the preparation for it!

Today, we take a car ride to the corner fast food restaurant, don't even have to get out of our seat, drive through and leave with a meal that we eat, usually in the car, on the way home. Or we eat an easy to prepare, prepackaged meal with preservatives and fats our body cannot figure out how to digest because they are not natural and then we go on with our fairly sedentary lives.

My point is that yes, they did fellowship around the table, but in order to get to that point, a lot of energy was spent through preparation. They probably spent the day walking around town, working in the marketplace, keeping the animals fed and healthy, they were active – not by choice, but by necessity. We do not have that necessity these days.

I saw an infomercial the other day that was selling a robotic gutter cleaner. What's going on? I was laughing at how ridiculous we've become. Imagine the calories you could burn by cleaning your gutters. Or, what about the sense of accomplishment you'd feel when you were all done? My guess is that the people who spend money on those robotic gutter cleaners will probably spend more time fixing the thing than they would have had to spend to actually get up and do the work themselves!

Boredom sends a lot of Americans to the refrigerator, too. We always feel like we have to be doing something. I imagine that is because we were made to move. Our bodies were designed to be productive, to get things done. In our society, we must schedule time for physical activity because our days are spent in a sedentary state. Do you think this is what God had planned?

Some Americans turn to food out of loneliness. This breaks my heart. I think the memories from childhood of the comforting effects of food sneak into the subconscious. We are falling for the lie that Satan tells us that the food will give us satisfaction we are missing in our lives.

We were created for one purpose – to worship God. When we were created, we were created with a God-shaped void, or hole. Some would describe this feeling as a feeling of emptiness. We were created this way so we would instinctively seek Him. Romans 1:20 says *"For since the creation of the world God's invisible qualities – his eternal power and divine nature – have been clearly seen, being understood from what has been made, so that men are without excuse"*.

This scripture tells that we were born with a sort of "God Radar" (if you will!). We are born into the sin of this world, but we seek His face, knowing instinctively that there is more to life than what is before us.

Satan's number one job is to distract us from finding Christ, at all costs. He distracts us with busyness, self-fulfillment, pride, doubt, legalism, hypocrites, addictions (alcohol, drugs, sex, food) *and even religion!* Oh, there are many other ways, but these are the ones that seem to be most obvious in today's world.

This emptiness in our soul cries out for God. We try filling it up by dependence on others, on status, on our addictions and even on our religions. Some people try to fill that void by looking "within themselves". I'm speaking of the new age movement – the lie that tells people that *you* are God and that you can be *self-fulfilled* and happy by looking within yourself. It's as if people are building a "tower of Babel" to God – brick by brick. Each lie that you believe will get you to God actually takes you further from Him. We all know what God did to the people who were building the tower of Babel, right? He scattered them all over the world and confused their language so they could not communicate with each other. Eventually, they gave up and realized they could not get to God this way (Genesis chapter 11 tells the story).

You cannot come to God by any other means than by having a relationship with Jesus Christ. My emptiness was filled the day I surrendered my life to Christ and gave Him complete control. Since that day, I've been a new creation. Paul said, in 1 Corinthians 5:17 *"Therefore, if anyone is in Christ, he is a new creation; the old has gone, the new has come!"* What a blessing to know that whoever I was before doesn't matter to God – all that matters is *whose* I am now.

CHAPTER FOUR

WHY ARE WE SO SILENT?

I was talking with a friend of ours, who is a pastor, about Body Builders and trying to get his views and thoughts on it. I told him I was going to be talking a lot of about the subject of gluttony and how God views it. When I said this, he said "Whoa! That's not an easy subject to go near"!

I wonder why we feel that gluttony is so difficult to discuss. It seems to be the "silent" sin. Just looking at the pulpit and seeing how many of our leaders struggle with obesity is disheartening. I believe the main reason it is not discussed is because once it's said out loud, everyone will be held accountable and not many people are willing to take on that responsibility. It's better to ignore it. Ignorance is bliss, right? **Wrong.**

We need to remember that sin is sin in God's eyes – no sin is worse than the other, it is all filthy in His sight. The thing that really disturbs me about gluttony is the physical effects it has on a human being. Obesity sneaks in after an abuse of food on the body, making one more vulnerable to disease, lack of confidence and lack of energy.

1 Corinthians 6:15 says *"Do you not know that your bodies are members of Christ Himself? Shall I then take the*

members of Christ and unite them with a prostitute? Never!"

Most Christians I know would never dream of uniting themselves with a prostitute (I hope!), but I believe the Apostle Paul was talking about any type of sin or perversion that enters the body, including gluttony. When we are thinking of over-indulging in food or drink, we need to remember that we are members of Christ Himself.

I'm certainly not saying that just because one is gluttonous that he or she is going to be obese. That's far from the truth! Some people are blessed with higher metabolism and some are born with slower metabolism. In speaking with a dear Christian friend of mine who struggles with her weight, she expressed something very profound to me. She said she often cries out to God and asks Him why she is faced with this particular struggle. She realizes, though, that it's a struggle that she cries out to God for and depends on His strength to get through it. That struck me in a way I had never thought of before.

In 1 Corinthians 12, Paul writes *"But he said to me, 'My grace is sufficient for you, for my power is made perfect in weakness' Therefore I will boast all the more gladly about my weaknesses, so that Christ's power may rest on me. That is why, for Christ's sake, I delight in weakness, in insults, in hardships, in persecutions, in difficulties. For when I am weak, then I am strong".*

My friend was expressing to me that she knew this was her weakness and that sometimes it makes her feel defeated. I know that *everyone* has something that brings them to their knees. There is not one person out there who doesn't know what it's like to struggle with a stronghold. ***Strongholds are an opportunity to rest in Him, to trust His guidance and a way for God to test our faith. They keep us humble.***

My friend's sister also struggles with food, but not with her weight. It was interesting to me, as I talked with both of them, how their struggles with food are so alike, but one did not show any physical "side effects". God makes each of us exactly how He chooses and He does not make mistakes. Just because we have a slower metabolism that doesn't mean we aren't exactly the person He created us to be. It means we must work a little harder. God never said it would be easy here on earth! But He did say time and time again that it would be *worth it!* The word "fight" is laced throughout the scriptures because that's what we must do – fight. But He gives us everything we need to prepare for the battle.

The sisters talked about how they get "giddy" when they think of eating something "bad". I know I get like that sometimes. "Oh, brownies - I know I shouldn't, but…!" seems to go through my head a lot. I'm not saying that you should never have a brownie – I am just saying you should keep food in it's proper perspective and as the scripture so beautifully states it in 1 Corinthians 10:23 *"Everything is permissible, but not everything is beneficial. Everything is permissible, but not everything is constructive"*. This scripture is referring to the law of love in relation to eating and drinking. I believe the key to keeping food in perspective is moderation – everything in moderation. When we start over-indulging, we are sinning.

The Bible is very consistent in letting us know that sin does not go unpunished. Numbers 32:23 says …*"you may be sure that your sins will find you out"*. I am reminded of the verse in 1 Timothy chapter 5 (verse 24) that says *"The sins of some men are obvious, reaching the place of judgment ahead of them"*. When I hear this verse, I think of someone who is struggling with obesity – someone who is turning to food for comfort and as a result, his or her body is showing the obvious effects of eating in excess. A lot of sins are done in secret, where nobody knows except God. But when we eat too much on a consistent basis, usually there is no hiding it.

That is why obesity is a disease that breaks my heart so

much – it's hard for anyone to admit they are living in sin (I struggled with my admission of alcoholism, and it wasn't even obvious to people) but when you are obese due to overeating, you cannot hide anything. Judgmental people are always willing to put in their two cents worth, making someone struggling with this disease even more ashamed. Satan loves that. That's why I think obesity is something he's been thrilled to see happening with more and more frequency.

I realize how difficult this subject is – I struggled myself with obesity. I know it's the most difficult thing in the world to try to break a habit that becomes such a part of who you are. **I also know that God is greater than any sin and with His help, this cycle can be broken.** 1 John 4:4 says *"the one who is in you is greater than the one who is in the world"*.

Nothing is impossible with God! In the Bible, Philippians 4:13 stresses that we can do ALL things through Christ, who strengthens us. That verse is not saying that we can do everything *except* conquer sin, but it is inclusive of this.

I do realize that some individuals have a genetic tendency to gain weight and store fat. Although not everyone with this tendency will become obese, some persons without genetic predisposition do become obese. Several genes have been identified as contributors to obesity, and researchers are constructing a human obesity gene map in hope of finding genetic targets in humans that may lead to the development of new treatments. But for the most part, the majority of obese people are that way because of poor food choices and lack of exercise.

I mentioned that because I don't want to seem insensitive to the people who are struggling with obesity that is directly related to their genetic makeup. It is very difficult for people with this tendency to lose weight, *but it is possible for them to be healthy.* When you look at scripture, you will realize that God actually enjoys making the impossible possible! He delights in using ordinary, everyday people to show His love, His power and His mercy.

If something seems impossible, think again. Faith is the key to unlocking God's healing power. God often wants to shower us with miracles, blessings and mercy – the problem comes from our unbelief, our inability to accept responsibility for our actions and our inactive prayer life.

God's word clearly says in Hebrews 10:22-25 *"Let us draw near to God with a sincere heart in **full assurance** of faith, having our hearts sprinkled to cleanse us from a guilty conscience and having our bodies washed with pure water. Let us not give up on meeting together, as some are in the habit of doing, but let us encourage one another – and all the more as you see the Day approaching."*

This is full assurance of forgiveness. That's the kind of faith we need to carry around with us. Something else you can pull from this verse is that second part where it says "let us not give up on meeting together". As Christians, we need to be supporting each other and encouraging each other in our faith.

If you are struggling with the sin of gluttony and are suffering from obesity as a result, please remember that all is not lost. I encourage you to start *today* by finding some Christian friends to surround and support you, increase your faith and pray for you and with you during your transition. Give it up to Christ and let Him guide you. Why carry around a burden that He's already carried and paid for?

We are on this earth to be the light of the world. That means we need to be energetic, ready and confident to be messengers of God's word. When we struggle with gluttony and obesity, Satan takes our confidence and rips it into little pieces and strips us of that energy we need to get through our days. It doesn't seem beneficial at all when you are in the midst of a struggle – you can sometimes feel over-whelmed. But keep in mind that God is sovereign and He will provide a way out.

> *1 Corinthians 10:13: No temptation has seized you except what is common to man. And God is faithful; he will not let you be tempted beyond what you can bear. But when you are tempted, he will also provide a way out so that you can stand up under it."*

When Paul says God will provide a way out, I realized that His provision was given when Jesus Christ died on that cross. Christ suffered every temptation known to man and yet He was sinless. We, too, are sinless in God's eyes once we are covered by Jesus' blood. We are free from sin! Romans 6:18 clearly states that *"You have been set free from sin and have become slaves to righteousness"*. That is our provision. We just need to reach out and accept it.

I have often thought, during the writing of this book, that I could actually just write one sentence that would sum it all up for us. Actually, this one sentence could be the answer to all of our problems and the summary of all the sermons preached in the world, all the seminars given on the Christian walk and it could change our world dramatically if everyone would heed it. Would you like to know what that sentence is?

Keep your eyes focused on Jesus Christ.

We get so focused on the sin in our lives that we lose sight of what matters – Jesus. That's it. It's really that simple. He paid the price for every sin we've ever commit-ted or ever will. I believe He did this so we could take that focus off the sin and just focus clearly on His plan for our lives. Why aren't we doing this?

We could sit around and beat ourselves up about the horrible things we've done and we could feel unworthy, but what kind of life would that be? Christ says *"The thief comes to destroy; I have come that they may have life, and have it more abundantly"*. Who do you think the "thief" in this passage is? Why, it's Satan of course. His whole existence is to make our existence anything *but* abundant!

Don't let him get that kind of stronghold in your life. If you are struggling with food, or anything else for that matter, you must realize that there is a way out. Yes, you may have to give up some things that are difficult to give up – things you thought you'd never be free from. I know what it's like to give up something I didn't think I'd ever be able to give up when I struggled with alcohol. It was nearly impossible for me to imagine a life without drinking. **Let's not ever, ever forget that God knows what it's like to give up something that seems unimaginable to give up – *He gave up His son!***

As a mother, I cannot even imagine giving up my son for anyone else. If I did, however, and they refused to accept the sacrifice, my heart would be deeply broken. When we refuse to accept Christ's provision for our sin, it must tear God's heart into pieces. He is the Way to an abundant life.

Let us not forget, either, that God is a just God. He can only take so much. When I first realized He wanted me to write this book, I was deep in prayer and He showed me something I cannot explain except to say that He is angry. He's angry with the state of Americans today. Not only are Americans denying God's presence more and more every day, but they are defiling *His Temple!* I don't know about you, but I don't want to experience God's wrath. Please, let's take His warnings seriously.

Paul doesn't mince words in 1 Corinthians 1:2 when he says *"Now it is **required** that those who have been given a* *trust must prove faithful"*. God has entrusted us with these bodies to do service for Him. When we are mistreating ourselves and it affects our confidence, our ability to witness or our health, we are not living up to our end of the deal. Romans 14:12 says *"So then, each one of us will give an account of himself to God"*. Does that verse scare you a little? If so, don't let it. You already have the power of God within you, just tap into it and reject the lifestyle that you might be struggling with that is holding you back. We need to be good stewards to that which God has entrusted to us.

Proverbs 23:21 says *"For drunkards and gluttons become poor, and drowsiness clothes them in rags.* Another verse in Proverbs (23:2) says *"Put a knife to your throat if you are given to gluttony"*. Those are pretty harsh words! It doesn't say *cut* your throat, but if a knife is held on your throat, that would sure make you think twice, wouldn't it? Let's clean out the temple instead of polluting it.

As you can see, I'm very passionate about this subject. I have researched the scripture and I've prayed about how to deliver this message and I hope that it is received in love.

CHAPTER FIVE

TRUTH OR CONSEQUENCES?

*Proverbs 28:23 "He who rebukes a man will
in the end gain more favor than he who has a
flattering tongue."*

When I first started instructing aerobics, I remember I was not very good at it. I did not know the beat of the music, I was very nervous (I threw up on the way to instructing my first class!) and I didn't have much confidence. Some people would lie to me and say that I was doing a great job – it was the best class they had ever taken – and then they'd leave and I'd never see them again.

Then there were the people who were honest with me – who saw my potential and decided it was better to help me along with truth than to allow me to embarrass myself by thinking I was really good because others were telling me so. I learned so much from these honest people. Yes, it's difficult to take constructive criticism, or correction, because it reminds us of our imperfections and it brings light to our weaknesses. But how are we to improve if we don't know what we need to improve upon?

If you are struggling with sin of any kind, whether it be

gluttony, self-centeredness, alcoholism, or anything else that seems insurmountable, it's better that someone be honest with you than for you to go around thinking you're fooling everyone. Don't you think it's more beneficial for you, in the long run, to know that someone cares about you enough to be honest? Sometimes it's hard to be honest with people because we don't want to make them unhappy or we don't want to seem like the "bad guy" in a situation.

The Bible paints true friends in a different light than that, though. Take Proverbs 27:6 for instance: *"Wounds from a friend can be trusted, but an enemy multiplies kisses."* So, it would seem that God delights in having friends express truth to one another, even if it means the one being told gets temporarily wounded by the truth. Ecclesiastes 4:10 says *"If one falls down, his friend can help him up. But pity the man who falls and has no one to help him up!"* or even Philippians 2:4 *"Each of you should look not only to your own interests, but also the interests of others."*

God is instructing us to be involved in each others' lives. We are to help each by offering correction, encouragement, instruction and our time. James 5:19 is very clear in this when James says *"My brothers, if one of you should wander from the truth and someone should bring him back, remember this: whoever turns a sinner from the error of his way will save him from death and cover a multitude of sins"*

The reason I bring all of this to light is because that is how I feel as I write this book. I do care, very much, that you all feel good after you read this book, and I do want you to feel uplifted, stronger and inspired while reading through the scriptures I've laced in the chapters. However, if you are feeling convicted for any reason, just know that is a good thing. **Conviction leads to repentance and repentance leads to Christ. We all know where Christ leads...to** *abundant life!!*

As I researched the subject of gluttony, I must confess

that I felt conviction, myself. In America, we are all guilty of this sin at one time or another (think THANKSGIV-ING!). I was saddened, though, to hear a brother in Christ from my church who is from Africa say that over in Africa, they don't even understand the meaning of overweight or obese. They look at Americans and shake their heads thinking they wish they just had enough food to share with their families to keep them alive. They cannot imagine a life like ours. That sure spoke to my heart.

As I looked over the statistics on obesity in America, I was shocked at how much it has increased through the years. It's a steady incline, too, and that worries me. We are a society of fast-food and "super-size", while we sit at desks and sit around the house watching television in our free time (if we have any at all). It's really not going to get better unless we take a stand.

I really believe God wants us to come together in the church and help each other through this. I know that God wants to do the seemingly impossible here! Churches need to unite on this and offer programs, education, accountability and even sermons on the sin of gluttony. **Let's quit sweeping it under the rug and bring it out of the darkness and into light**.

The day we accepted Christ, we stepped out of the darkness and into the light! Things are made obvious in the light and we should not be ashamed of who we are, regardless of the sin we may or may not have committed. We can take our experiences and grow from them, helping others learn along the way. Jesus took our shame on the cross. Don't be afraid to admit your shortcomings. You'd be surprised how many people out there are in the exact same situation as you are – or even worse. Don't be afraid of the accountability either, it's a *good thing!*

Sometimes, we even have difficulty in receiving constructive criticism from ourselves! When I was struggling with alcohol, I was doing it in complete secret and I even denied it to myself. As I stepped into the light and revealed to those around me what I had been hiding for so long, I think I shocked them. When people think of an alcoholic, they think of someone who wakes up and drinks, has a brown bag with them all the time and cannot get it together. I was together (or so it seemed) on the outside, but I was a slave to alcohol.

As a mom with four children and a husband who was working 80 hours per week (at least), by the time 5:00pm would come around, I would be completely stressed out and rather than resting in Christ and depending on Him for strength, I would drown myself in alcohol to numb my stress and my loneliness. Yes, my flesh is embarrassed to admit this and my human side doesn't like people to know about it because it is not something I'm proud of, *but in order to be able to be used by God, I must confess it and try to be there to help others who might be hiding in sin and they feel trapped.* I needed to be honest with myself about my situation. Once I did, I was able to give it to God, admit my weakness and depend on His strength.

In 1 Peter 2:9 Paul says *"But you are a chosen people, a royal priesthood, a holy nation, a people belonging to God, that you may declare the praises of him who called you out of darkness into his wonderful light".* He goes on to say in verse 11: *"Dear friends, I urge you, as aliens and strangers in the world, to abstain from sinful desires, which wage war against your soul. Live such good lives among the pagans that, though they accuse you of doing wrong, they may see your good deeds and glorify God on the day he visits us".*

The scripture goes on to talk about how when we do good and overcome sin, people who do not believe and who want to put us down for our faith are silenced. This is God's way of showing His presence in our lives without us having to say a word. The silent witness is such an effective one!

When we start trying to do the work of the Holy Spirit, though, we start getting ourselves into trouble. If you see someone who is struggling with sin, yes we are responsible to help them as brothers and sisters in Christ, but we cannot go on the attack. It is the Holy Spirit's work to convict, not ours. We can pray for them, show them in our actions, or deliver the scripture in love but we must allow the Holy Spirit to work in them. We should never try to pressure people into making a decision or a change.

It's your duty to live a life that makes them see that you are different. That, alone, will make them curious and then you may even be approached by them. And pray. Pray a lot – asking God to reveal to you how to approach the situation and asking Him to use you to help them. Believe me, a prayer like that, prayed sincerely from the heart, will be an effective prayer that God will want to answer.

Correction is something that is difficult to accept in the flesh. As we become more mature in Christ and more like Him, we see that it gets a little easier. Correction seems painful at the time, but the Bible is filled with scripture that talks about how important it is. Proverbs 29:15 says *"The rod of correction imparts wisdom"*. Proverbs 12:1 says *"Whoever hates correction is stupid"*. Proverbs 15:15 says *"Whoever heeds correction shows prudence."* And the list goes on. We grow through correction! We become more like Christ, and that should be our goal.

This is why I believe that attending a Bible-based church is essential for Christian growth. I spoke with a sweet lady the other day who wants to grow as a Christian, but she feels that "saved" people were judgmental, holier than thou and rude so she does not want to go to church. I explained to her how important it is to fellowship with other Christians, and that maybe she just hadn't found the right church yet. I told her I would pray for her and her husband to find a church that would love them as Christ does. She was so grateful for that.

If you are currently seeking a church, please remember that churches are made up of imperfect people. Sometimes, when people look for a church, they scare away at the first sign of sin or imperfection. The person who is looking for a perfect church will be sorely disappointed! You must search the scriptures, pray and ask God for direction. He will lead you to where He wants you to be, and that's a promise.

So many people are turned off from churches who try to do the work of the Holy Spirit. You know the churches – the ones with leaders who try to convict with fire and brimstone sermons every Sunday, who have meetings to discuss how sinful the congregation is, but never take the time to look in the mirror and consider their own sin. If you find yourself in a place like this, please know that is not God's plan. We are told to love each other, offer correction and pray – not to wound each other through judgmental, unkind words.

This makes me think of the story in John, chapter 8 where the teachers of the law (Pharisees) brought a woman before Jesus who had been caught committing adultery. They wanted to stone her to death for her sin. They stood in judgment of her, not willing to forgive. Jesus said to them (in verse 7) *"If anyone of you is without sin, let him be the first to throw a stone at her"*. Of course, there was no one there who had not sinned, so eventually everyone left and the only two people left there were Jesus and the woman. Jesus told her she was not condemned, so she should go and *sin no more.*

Now if Jesus can forgive and forget, why is it that we have such a difficult time forgiving? Find a church that supports and loves you, offers correction in a loving way and prays. That is definitely God's plan!

When I ask people what are some of the best qualities in your best friend, nine times out of ten they say that they like that their friend is honest with them. As you fill your life with Christian friends, always look to Jesus as an example of how to be a friend to those around you. Just like when you are looking for a church, you need to surround yourself with people who support and love you, offer correction and pray.

*"Blessed is the man whom **God** corrects" Job 5:17*

CHAPTER SIX

PAUSE FOR THE CAUSE

As I was driving to a business function yesterday, I was running a little late. I was on a busy highway and I was in the right lane because I knew my exit was coming up. As I drove, I came up behind this big white Cadillac with an elderly couple in the two front seats. They were going a steady 40 miles per hour. Ugh.

My first reaction was to put my turn signal on and try to get around them as quickly as possible, but I saw cars just racing past me and I knew my car couldn't find a place to fit into that race, so I just resided myself to wait behind the Cadillac until my exit.

My heart was racing and I was getting more impatient by the minute. What was wrong with these people? Did they even deserve to be on the road? My flesh was starting to take over. Then I heard the Father's soft voice speak to me. I knew right away that God was using this moment to teach me something, so I started paying attention.

I looked at the elderly couple in the car. They were so happy! Happy to be alive, happy to still be able to drive and get around and they seemed to really be taking in the sights along side of the road. I imagined they were probably taking notice of all the leaves that were turning orange, yellow and brown in the trees. I imagined they were listening to music that helped lift their spirits as they traveled a frighteningly unfamiliar piece of road in their Cadillac.

Then I looked at the 3 lanes to my left. People were flying by at top speed, talking on cell phones, eating, hurried and determined to get to their next destination. They didn't even notice the leaves, I thought. They were honking their horns as if to tell the sweet older gentleman to get off the road (yes, now that I could see the elderly couple as God sees them, they captured my heart)! I wanted to defend them. I wanted to protect their world that seemed so peaceful and joyful. Then I realized that just a few seconds before this thought had come to me, I was one of "them" in the other lanes.

At that moment, I had tears forming in my eyes as I thanked God for taking an everyday situation and making it into a teachable moment for me. I felt so blessed by that sweet older couple. Their ability to pause and take in each moment is something to cherish. In our society, we find this very difficult.

If you are struggling with the sin of gluttony, or any other stronghold for that matter, try looking at this struggle as a teachable moment from God. Because that's exactly what it is. He wants you to learn something from your own unique experience and as you learn more about what He wants you to learn, you will be able to bless Him by glorifying Him, regardless of your circumstance.

In my church's spiritual gifts class, I learned a lot about my personality. It was interesting how they can make a test and they totally nailed my personality, trait for trait, without ever having met me! I was convinced someone had followed me around and taken notes or something. Really, it sort of blew my mind.

One thing I learned though is that someone with a

personality like mine (excitable, energetic, passionate, idea-focused, but not so great at follow through) really needs to take time to pause. That's not something I do easily. That would probably be why I have a struggle with patience. Satan wants to distract me and throw me off track. So I've realized that in order to live my life for Christ effectively, I need to *pause for the cause*. Pausing and realizing that God wants to use a situation to teach me something is a whole new thought process for me.

This could work for you, too. Instead of focusing on how difficult it seems to overcome obstacles or sin in your life, realize that you have this struggle for a purpose. **You have two choices – you can succumb to the sin and face the consequences or you can rise above it, learn from it, and live victoriously through Christ.**

God wants us to call on Him in a time of crisis. Do you call on Him at a time of distress? Did you know that when you do not call on Him that it actually grieves Him? *You actually deny Him glory when you turn from Him and try to fix things for yourself.* Sometimes He allows you to reach a place of need so you will call on Him and others around you can see Him at work in your life.

Think of it this way, if you didn't have any struggles at all, you would reach a place in your life where you would become self-sufficient. *Christians are Christ-sufficient!* Christ says in John 15:7 *"If you remain in me and my words remain in you, ask whatever you wish and it will be given you. This is my Father's glory, that you bear much fruit, showing yourselves to be my disciples."*

Christ wants to help us! It brings the Father glory when we call on Him and as a result of our calling on Him, we can show bear much fruit and show Christ to others.

I don't know what your stronghold is, but I'm certain you have one. **We all have something that brings us to our knees.** I want to encourage you to seek God's guidance as you deal with it and realize that as you overcome strongholds, Satan is ready to pounce on you with a replacement - I can testify to this!

Once I finally overcame my gluttony, I struggled with alcohol. Once I overcame alcohol, I was faced with frustration. Once I overcame frustration, I was faced with impatience. There are times that gluttony rears its ugly head, alcohol brings temptation and frustration is usually something I still must struggle with frequently. Impatience, well, that's my current stronghold! The strongholds never fully go away, but they get easier as you learn that Christ has overcome them all – and as you depend on Him to overcome them, your struggles will seem less wearisome.

I'm the kind of person who needs discipline in my life if I'm going to be successful at anything because by nature I'm not an extremely disciplined person. When I decided, with God's leading, to write this book, I knew it would take discipline. Not to write, that's the easy part, but to *pause* and let God speak to me. Once I start something, I don't want to stop until I'm completely finished or I feel like it's something I have "hanging over my head".

But the Holy Spirit made it perfectly clear that I was going to be learning something very valuable in this process. I cannot explain how, but I just know that God wants me to spend no more than an hour a day on this book. I promised Him I would do just that. I, of course, have run across some times when I kept trying to write because I felt I was on a "roll", but God would not allow me to go past my hour!

When I go past my hour, I am spent. I cannot think straight, the words do not come and I feel like the Holy Spirit just stops "pouring into me". That's a Father's discipline, in a loving way, to help me walk away from the project and leave it unfinished while He speaks to me until the next day when I can sit down and share my thoughts for another hour.

It's taught me a lot – it's taught me that I can, indeed, walk away from a project that is not completely finished, come back and the world will not end as a result! It's taught me that pausing to take time to hear God's instruction is essential. Come to think of it, aren't we all just God's unfinished projects, anyway?

Pause for the Cause. It's going to change your life. What is God teaching you through your current struggle? Call upon the Lord and wait patiently upon Him to rescue you. Then give Him the glory that He deserves!

Psalm 50:15 "Call upon Me in the day of trouble; I will deliver you, and you shall glorify me".

CHAPTER SEVEN

"CROSS" TRAINING

"For physical training is of some value, but godliness has value for all things, holding promise for both the present life and the life to come". 1 Timothy 4:8

When I read that verse, it reminds me about perspective. We need to keep things in their proper perspective. A lot of the reason I am writing this book is to bring light to the importance of physical fitness within the church body, but I cannot discuss the importance of this aspect without showing what is even more important.

I know a lot of Christians who do not place much emphasis on the health and fitness of their physical bodies, but they are spiritually nourished and thriving. Apparently, in the preceding verse, Paul is saying spiritual training is more important than physical – and I must agree. When we are trained in godliness, we are much more effective for God's purposes. When we are truly spiritually fit, we have a desire to please God in every way, even by being fit in our physical bodies.

What is interesting is that physical training is of *some*

value. It is valuable enough that Paul mentioned it. Paul even recognized, back in the days when physical fitness was a way of life, not something to be "fit in" to one's day that it was important. We, too, should see that it's important and take steps to get more active and feel healthier.

So where does mental and emotional fitness fit into all of this? Let me give you an example of mental fitness in my life (or should I say "lack of?"). When I was struggling with exercise bulimia, I was convinced in my mind that I was fat and ugly. I remember looking in the mirror thinking that even though people would tell me how thin I looked, I did not see that person in the mirror.

My mind had completely convinced me that something that was totally untrue was true and that everyone was against me. It took me to a place of constant fear and constant self-evaluation. I was so focused on that aspect of my life, that it left little or no room for anything else. This is how Satan works. He is the master of confusion. He can take your mind to places you'd never dream of going and convince you that something that is not true is truth. He can manipulate you into believing everyone is looking at you, everyone wants you to fail, people don't love you, God is not real and that you are not worthy.

Mental fitness is so important. When we see someone who struggles with, for instance, anxiety, that is a clear picture of how powerful the mind is. I have suffered from severe anxiety attacks in my past. At one point, I fell on my mom's couch and completely blacked out, while saying the Lord's Prayer. She had to call an ambulance for me, and when they took my pulse it was at 180 beats per minute. My blood pressure was something like 190/110. There was absolutely nothing wrong with me, but I had convinced myself that I was going to die, so my body went into a sort of "shock". I still feel myself sometimes going into that "place" of anxiety, and just as I start to slip into it, I say to myself "Leslie, you have a choice. You can give in and 'go there' or you can overcome this with the power of Christ and walk away from it". I have not had a single attack since I've started using that approach. You see, in 1 Corinthians 2:16 it says *"But we have the mind of Christ."* I am no longer a slave to this mental prison – I'm free because Christ has set me free.

I realize that some people take medications for anxiety, and I want you to know that I'm truly convinced that if it helps you, you should remain on the medication. That just might be the way that God has chosen to heal you. I am not anti-medication, and I certainly do not believe that God heals everyone in the same way, so if you are suffering from anything that requires medication, just remember that in 1 Timothy, chapter 5 verse 23, Paul said to Timothy (who had some stomach problems) *"Stop drinking only water and use a little wine because of your stomach and frequent illnesses"*. They did not have medications as we do today back then, and the water was not purified like we are able to get today, so in order to kill off bacteria, they used wine as a medication. Paul was telling Timothy that it's okay to use medication. It's obviously one of God's provisions.

So, just as people with poor eyesight use glasses, people with no hair use wigs or toupees, people with allergies use anti-histamines and people with hunger pangs use food, remember that all good things come from God and He gives us provisions. So don't feel like your faith is not strong enough to heal you, because God provides healing in many different ways.

I would like to show you a positive side of mental and emotional fitness. When we are convinced that we have purpose, have a mission and we are right with God, we are given a whole new mental outlook on life. When Christ takes over, something wonderful happens – we become free from being a slave to the world because now we are a slave to Christ and His purpose.

When we are in check spiritually, our emotions and mentality can directly affect the way we treat our bodies. The way we treat our bodies is an outward reflection of how we feel about ourselves. Do you see how they all tie in now?

Now, I also recognize that there are Christians who are in the gym 5 times a week, but never in the Word of God. It is not recommend that Christians put physical fitness in a higher priority than spiritual nourishment. I've tried this before, and I promise you it will not put you in a place where you will be able to be used by God the way He wants to use you.

The single most important thing you can do for yourself is to be spiritually fit. David says in Psalm 119:105 *"Thy word is a lamp unto my feet and a light unto my path"*. It gives us direction, helps us to live the way God wants us to live and it is life's perfect Instruction Manual. Living without God's Word is living a life with no direction, no instruction, no correction and it puts you in a situation where sin can easily penetrate you. *Spiritual accountability is reached through studying God's Word.*

If we are physically fit, as I stated in earlier chapters, you will be more productive, more confident and more energetic. Being accountable to God for your physical fitness might be the answer to your inability to be motivated to be active. Ask Him for guidance, direction and accountability. A great idea would be to find a friend to come alongside of you (a Christian friend would be ideal – someone you can pray with and for).

Alignment is the key here. If you feel you do not have time for your spiritual, emotional, physical or mental fitness and development, then you must reexamine your schedule and prioritize. Do you need to wake up earlier? Do you need to cut some things that aren't necessary out of your schedule?

Do you need to surround yourself with more positive people who share your values? God wants you to be fit – physically, mentally, emotionally and spiritually.

You will be amazed at how useful you will be to God and how much He can accomplish through you when you have energy and confidence. You must stay connected through His Word and communicate with Him daily through prayer.

Before you make a decision about something – whether to exercise or not, whether to read a book or not, whether to eat a second helping or not – you need to ask yourself the question *"If I do this, will it lead me to a place where I can glorify God?"* If the answer is no, you should re-think the activity. If the answer is yes, you know what you should do.

Remember that once you become a Christian, *it's **not** about you anymore!* John the Baptist said it best when he said in John 3:30 *"He (Jesus) must become greater; I must become less"*. We are here to live for Christ and we need to make decisions that reflect Him and His purposes, not us and our purposes. Romans 8:5 clearly states *"Those who live according to the sinful nature have their minds set on what the nature desires; but those who live in accordance with the Spirit have their minds set on what the Spirit desires"*.

When I see that verse, the part that says "in accordance with the Spirit" tells us that we need to consult God about every decision we make and He will lead us in the right direction. We need to consider **"Will this activity fulfill my flesh-derived desires or God's spiritual desires for my life"**? When we can master this way of living and making decisions, we can live in harmony between mind, body and spirit.

That brings me to something that's been on my heart lately: the relationship between our minds, emotions, bodies and spirits. I initially had a triangle in mind, with one side representing mind, one side body and the other spirit.

However, a dear friend of mine pointed out that there might be something to learn by looking at the cross of Jesus. As I prayed about it and searched for the answer, it came to me during my quiet time.

The cross of Jesus represents so much. Here are some of the representations that come to mind:

- *Sacrifice:* Jesus sacrificed His life for us so we could live abundant life.
- *Completeness:* Jesus said in John 19:30 *"It is finished."* Nothing more needed to be done – everything was in alignment.
- *Love:* Jesus was a man full of emotion. Emotions are a good thing! Jesus wept, Jesus laughed, Jesus was righteously angry, Jesus loved more than any human who ever walked the earth and He proved that love on the cross.
- *Devotion:* Jesus was completely devoted to His Purpose and nothing would deter him from achieving it, not Satan, not fear, not people's opinions and not even His disciples.
- *Oneness:* The cross represents oneness with Christ because when we cast our cares and burdens on the cross and accept Jesus as Lord of our lives, we become one with Him and we then share in His Kingdom and Purpose (2 Corinthians 5:18).

So in relation to our own bodies, which we know are the temple of the Holy Spirit, we can make a very strong comparison. Our bodies, through the cross, can become the body God intended for us to have if we focus on the picture of what the cross actually represents in relation to our bodies:

- *Sacrifice:* We must make sacrifices in order to be able to achieve the goals that God puts before us. Sacrifices are tough, but God always gives back so much more than we give up!

- **Completeness:** In order to have Complete Fitness, we must recognize that we need to nurture our bodies, our minds, our spirit and our emotional health. We can do our best for God's purposes when we are complete.
- **Love:** This is a tough one for some of us. Love is the first commandment. We are to love the Lord our God with all of our heart, soul, strength and mind. And secondly, we are to love our neighbor *as ourselves.* Do you love yourself? Do you realize that if you do not, you are not capable of loving others the way God wants you to? Love is an emotion we cannot afford to live without. Emotions are something we need to nurture.
- **Devotion:** Have you surrendered your body and your life to Christ? You must be fully devoted to His Purpose for you. Believe me, you have a purpose. You were created for big things! Pray and seek God's will for your life – your big dream. What have you always wanted to do? What would you do if fear of failure or fear of leaving your comfort zone was not an issue? *Do it.* Devote yourself to this purpose and give it to the Lord and you will achieve great things. He has provided everything you need, you just need to accept it and give Him your life.
- **Oneness:** You must become one with Christ if you want to be in complete alignment. We are incapable of achieving true success without His leading. We might look successful to the outside world, but inside we will always be searching for something more. You get one chance to live this life, a life I consider to be a test run for the life to come. Don't waste it by living for self. Live your life for Christ!

The next time you feel overwhelmed about what you need to do in order to achieve Complete Fitness, I strongly recommend you look to the cross. I like to refer to it as "Cross" Training! Here is a visual picture for you:

BODY

MIND   EMOTIONS

SPIRIT

Our spiritual fitness represents the Holy Spirit's role in our lives and is the base – the foundation of how sturdy the "cross" is. If you pour a concrete foundation, that cross isn't going anywhere! So, we see how important that base is.

The mind and emotions are represented by Christ, who came to earth and actually felt the exact same emotions you and I face every day. When we accept Christ as our Savior, Paul tells us in 1 Corinthians 2:16 *"But we have the mind of Christ"*.

The body represents God, as we are created in His Image (Genesis 1:26). The trinity is represented beautifully in our own existence. God is such an amazing and wonderful God! We owe him everything and as we draw closer to Him, we realize that it's such an honor to give up our lives for His Purpose!

Paul tells us to offer our bodies as a living sacrifice, holy and pleasing to God because this is our spiritual act of worship (Romans 12:1). There can be no question that it is imperative that we understand the importance of Complete Fitness – not too *look better* as much as it is to *be better.*

I guess you can tell that throughout the book I've referred a lot to Paul's writings in the New Testament. He just really touches my heart with his honesty, his willingness to correct in love, and his accomplishments, despite his past.

Paul (known as Saul before his conversion) was a Jewish man who persecuted Christians constantly. God saw something in Paul though and Christ revealed Himself to him on the side of the road on the way to Damascus (where he was going to persecute and even kill some Christians). Acts chapter 9 beautifully portrays the conversion of Saul (who later became Paul). I highly recommend you put this book down and read this story right now – it's truly beautiful and it gives a wonderful picture of God's power to convert even the most sinful of men!

The reason I bring this up is because I know that Paul took his "spiritual fitness" very seriously. He spent many years studying God's word in Arabia and Damascus before going up to Jerusalem to get acquainted with Peter. (See Galatians chapter 1 verses 13-24). He wanted to be used by God in a mighty way, but before he could do that, he knew he had to study, learn and just be still enough to listen to God's calling and direction before heading out into the ministry.

For much of America, it's all about hurrying up and going. Christians are sometimes very hasty to get involved once they experience salvation because they want to shout it from the rooftops! It's good to feel this way, and God *can and will* use us immediately, but take time to get to understand why you believe what you believe and learn how to defend your faith by digging in deep to God's word.

Sometimes God just wants us to be like Mary in Luke

Chapter 10 when she sat there at Christ's feet while Martha was busy getting things done (I referred to this story in a previous chapter). Martha says to Jesus *"Lord, don't you care that my sister has left me to do all the work by myself? Tell her to help me!* And Jesus replied *"Martha, Martha, you are worried and upset about many things, but only one thing is needed. Mary has chosen what is better and it will not be taken away from her"*.

He wants us to take that time to learn, to be fed and to really get to know Him. When we do this, He will bless us and give us a vision for His Kingdom. But if we neglect our Spiritual life, we will never be able to experience the true joy that comes from knowing God's will for our lives and the true joy that comes from being used by God to fulfill His purpose.

In a football game, you play hard, but then you get time outs and a full-blown half-time to re-think your strategy, get new ideas, encourage each other and rest before playing again. Think of time at Jesus' feet as a "time out" or even a "half time" (depending on your need). It's a much needed time to strategize, get encouraged, learn something and *rest*. Once you are ready, believe me God, the Ultimate Coach, will be calling you back into the game, so it's a good idea to be ready when that time comes by being as fit as you can possibly be.

CHAPTER EIGHT

I'LL START ON MONDAY

Why do today what you can put off until tomorrow? That seems to be the thinking of most people in America. We are living in a continual state of "tomorrow" and for most of us, that tomorrow rarely comes.

What's the first thing you do when you decide to start exercising or go on a diet? You say "I'll start Monday", right? Why is that? We put off things that are uncomfortable, things that take us out of our comfort zones, because we would prefer to be in our comfy, cozy state of denial for as long as possible.

There are many reasons people procrastinate. Some of those reasons are personality types, fear of failure, fear of rejection, fear of embarrassment, lack of willpower, lack of energy, lack of discipline and just plain laziness. None of these reasons are insurmountable, and as we know, nothing is impossible with God.

Lack of time is another reason. I have heard many people say that they just don't have enough time in their day to be physically active, to pray or to read the Bible. We all have the same amount of minutes, hours and seconds in our day it's just that we all prioritize our time according to what is important to us. If physical fitness is not important to you, you won't spend time working on it. So, the question really isn't if you have the time or not, it's really the question of how much it means to you.

Just remember, *fitness does not take time out of your life, it puts life into your time.* It puts a whole new perspective on it when we realize this. What if Noah had procrastinated building the ark? What if Jonah *had not* procrastinated going to Nineveh? What if when God told Moses to part the sea, he said "You know, God, I'm kind of busy and I could really use a nap, how about tomorrow?" Procrastination is *never* from God and can only result in discipline from God as a result of our disobedience. Do it *now!*

Recently, I struggled with procrastination myself. I was feeling very called by God to go out and minister to women's groups, church groups and youth groups about the sin of gluttony, the benefits of Complete Fitness, "Cross" Training and the basic Biblical truths that I write about in this book.

However, I was almost paralyzed with fear at the thought of doing this. I knew it's what God called me to do, but I felt a sense of fear at the mere thought of the possibility of failure. What if I made a mistake? What if I said something stupid? What if, just like in my personal interview at the Mrs. United States pageant, my mouth dries up like the Sahara Desert and I cannot speak because my tongue would be stuck to the roof of my mouth and white stuff starts forming in the corners? Oh, and the worst of all, what if there are people there who are smarter, more Christian, more theological and more spiritual that I am and they disagree with something I say?

I felt like a race car that was sitting at the start line. For years, my race car just sat there, while all the other cars passed me by. I collected dust, and never even tried to turn over the engine. Now that I've surrendered my life, my car is finally cleaned up and it looks great! When I was writing the book and preparing my seminar, I felt I was turning over the engine. When I found a publisher, I felt like my engine was actually running and I even pushed on the gas a few times to show my enthusiasm.

However, in order to take it out of park and get into the race, I must let go of my fear and realize that God has called me for a purpose. Yes, there will be mistakes. Yes, knowing me, I'll say something stupid every now and then (I'm convinced God finds that endearing about me!). Yes, there will be people who may not agree with everything I say. But I cannot let that stop me from doing what God is calling me to do, because that would be disobedience. Disobedience leads to the woodshed, and I don't want to go there! More than that though, disobedience hinders blessing, and I know I will be blessed if I follow God's will for my life and more importantly, *I will bless Him.*

Sure, my race car can still go with the parking break on, so maybe I could just hold on to some of my fear? No way. Once I completely bind the spirit of fear, in the name of Jesus, I can go full steam ahead and I can accomplish everything God wants for me in my race without falling behind.

Is your car cleaned up? Is your engine on? Are you riding with the parking break on? If you are struggling with procrastination, I hope you understand that God made you to accomplish *today* what you have been putting off for tomorrow. We are not promised tomorrow! There are three things I want people to remember about me when I die. Those three things are that I loved God with everything in me, that I loved and adored my family and that I followed my dreams, no matter how foolish people thought I was or how strong the possibility of failure was. What do you want people to remember about you?

I say this is the day you begin whatever it is that you've been putting off. Maybe it's a project, maybe it's a ministry, or maybe, just maybe it's a lifestyle change? I encourage you to keep reading, keep studying and keep searching for God's will for your life.

Isaiah 55:6 says *"Seek the Lord while he may be found; call on him while he is near"*. Now that verse doesn't say "seek the Lord tomorrow, because he'll always be there", does it? The biggest mistake someone can make in their life is to procrastinate when it comes to making a decision to follow the Lord.

A preacher once told the story about a man who was in his congregation during a revival. It was one of those old fashioned, tent revivals and there were a lot of people there who were not regular church members. One guy really stood out to the preacher. He was in about the fifth row and he seemed very on edge and uncomfortable throughout the revival. During the invitation, the preacher asked if anyone wanted to make a decision to follow Christ, that they could come forward and say the prayer of salvation with one of the volunteers at the front. He looked up and saw the man with his head bowed, crying, but clutching so tightly onto the chair in front of him that his knuckles turned white.

The gentleman never did come forward, but the preacher went up to him once the service was over and asked if he needed to talk about anything, or if he could share more information about Jesus with him. The man wouldn't even look the preacher in the eyes and turned away saying "I'm not ready, I'll come back on Sunday and maybe we'll talk then". That night, on the way home, the man was in an automobile accident and lost his life. The tragedy of all of this is the fact that he had a chance to make a decision for Christ, but he thought he had all the time in the world. He will be separated from Christ for eternity now. This is procrastination at its worst.

If you are struggling with your weight, with sin, with a decision to follow Christ or with anything that you've been putting off, just know that today is the day you can change your life. It's hard to make change, I know. I remember thinking that if I surrendered my life to Christ that would mean I would have to give up some things that I didn't think I could live without. When we turn to Christ, though, we are a new creation and our desires change. I am no longer living to please Leslie I'm living to please Christ.

2 Peter 1:5-8 says *"...make every effort to add to your faith goodness; and to goodness, knowledge; and to knowledge,* **self-control;** *and to self control,* **perseverance;** *and to perseverance, godliness; and to godliness, brotherly kindness; and to brotherly kindness, love.* **For if you possess these qualities in increasing measure, they will keep you from being ineffective and unproductive** *in your knowledge of our Lord Jesus Christ"*

Get your race car running and get into the race. Don't sit on the sidelines any longer – God's plans for you are so much more! Begin by seeking God's will for your life and then doing whatever you can to accomplish what it is He wants you to do. You'll never be able to accomplish your dreams if you are so behind in tomorrows that you can't even remember what the dream was in the first place.

CHAPTER NINE

WALKING IN CONFIDENCE

Today I was running on the local sidewalk with the sun to my back. I use my time of exercising to pray, search for God's guidance and to listen to praise music. As I jogged along the sidewalk, I noticed my shadow right before me. I would try to pray, but I kept getting distracted by my shadow. I would look at my outline and think "Gee, my legs look so big" or "I am jiggling a lot according to my shadow – I hope people driving by don't notice".

I kept getting distracted and could not, for the life of me, get a clear "line" to God. I was praying He would reveal Himself to me in some way, would show me something I could apply to my life, but I was getting nothing. Just as I was about to get totally discouraged, I decided it was time to turn around and go home.

Just as I was turning around, one of my favorite songs was playing on my CD player – the song "Everywhere" by Third Day. The verse that was playing was the one that says "*Like the sun upon my face, I feel the warmth of your embrace – you are everywhere*". I immediately felt the warm sun on my face and could just feel the Holy Spirit's embrace as I started jogging back home.

The Lord was revealing a lot of great things to me – answering some tough questions, giving me peace about some issues in my life that I'd been struggling with and I just felt a warmth and openness that I longed for. A few minutes later, I realized that my shadow was gone. It was behind me now, not in front of me. The Holy Spirit was lovingly showing me that when I take my eyes off of myself and focus on Him, then that gives Him the power to work in my life. No shadow to distract me, no self-doubt, just God. It was a beautiful revelation and one that I will never forget!

The world is very outward focused. It is so easy to get sucked into that kind of thought-process, and that is exactly what Satan wants us to do. I have spent the good part of my life worrying about my looks, worrying about wrinkles, imperfections and gaining or losing weight. Who is perfect anyway? I can't think of one person who has it all together. I mean, have you *ever* heard someone say "I'm the perfect size, and I'm smart, fun to be around and my wrinkles are the most attractive thing I've ever seen!"?

I was at a conference last week and something very interesting happened. I walked into a class that was set aside for the elite, the highly educated people who were attending the conference. I believe they referred to it as the "masters" class. Anyway, when I told my husband I was going to that class he said "Why? You aren't a master yet – are you supposed to go to this class? Is it appropriate?" My answer was probably naïve, but I was honestly just interested in what the speaker was speaking on – it was about passion and how to recognize your passion and it didn't matter to me that it was for the "masters" because, by golly, it's what I wanted to learn about.

As I entered the class, I looked around at some of the most intimidating, stuffy people I'd ever seen. I began to second-guess myself. Did I deserve to be there? What if they could tell by looking at me that I'm not a master?

Would I fit in? As I sat in my chair, the speaker started to introduce herself and she asked us to divide into groups and talk about what we fear most and how that's holding us back from what we want to accomplish. She shared her greatest fear with us right off the bat – it was that everyone in the room would somehow realize, during her presentation, that she is a fraud.

Immediately I felt a connection with this woman. I really appreciated her authenticity and her willingness to admit a fear that apparently was something she really struggled with. It all came back to confidence. And if an instructor of "masters" was feeling this way, it made me realize that we all have a common bond, no matter how educated or uneducated we are. Confidence got her on that stage, though, despite her fears, and her ability to connect with us on such a personal level really made me realize that we all have issues with confidence no matter how "wise" the world says we are. Some people are just better at pretending than others!

My biggest challenge from being a Christian has come from accepting my identity in Christ, not in what others think of me. I needed to turn from "self" confidence to "God" confidence. I read in *The Ancient Paths* by Craig S. Hill that when you take what someone else thinks of you as truth, when you base your identity on what others think of you, you are putting them in a position of God in your life and that is a form of idolatry. This blew my mind and it changed the way I looked at my life. This book, by the way, is awesome and it truly helps you understand how the ancient paths that God has established are a key to living a God-filled life.

People often look at the Ten Commandments and when they come across the "Thou shalt not have any other gods before me", they imagine a golden calf or maybe some other man-made or self-proclaimed god. But anything you esteem over the Lord is an idol. I esteemed others' opinions more than I esteemed God's. That was idolatry. Can you relate?

I hear the term "self esteem" a lot these days. It's important people feel good about them selves, so don't get me wrong here. I am all for feeling good. However, when we put our confidence or our esteem in our selves, we get into trouble. Our confidence should come from God and our esteem should be for Him alone. It saddens me to see others struggle with their identity – especially Christians. Our identity is totally based on Christ from the moment He is invited into our lives.

When we put our confidence in our flesh, it's like we are paying more attention to our shadows than we are the sun (or Son) that is making that shadow possible. Our bodies are not perfect, our lives are not perfect and once we become Christians, we are still not promised a perfect, easy life. If we put our confidence in things that are not eternal, we will become discouraged, disillusioned and eventually we will lose sight of our eternal purpose. In the book of 2 Corinthians 4:18 it says *"So we fix our eyes not on what is seen, but on what is unseen. For what is seen is temporary, but what is unseen is eternal"*.

1 Peter 4:9-10 says *"But you are a **chosen people, a royal priesthood, a holy nation, a people belonging to God,** that you may declare the praises of him who called you out of darkness into his wonderful light. Once you were not a people, but now **you are the people of God;** once you had not received mercy; but now **you have received mercy.**"*

Let's see, we are
- A chosen people
- Royal priests
- A holy nation
- Belonging to God
- People of God
- Receivers of mercy

- Called out of darkness into His wonderful light

It sounds like God thinks pretty highly of us. Not because of anything we've done, mind you, but because of what Christ did for us and because we've chosen to accept that awesome gift.

I once heard a speaker at a conference say this: **The next time you are faced with a condemning thought like "I'm fat" or "I'm not good enough", tack on your identity to the end of the sentence. Say ....*in Christ* after each condemnation.** "I'm fat *in Christ*" sure doesn't sound like something God would want us to say, does it? Or "I'm not good enough *in Christ*" – well, that just sounds impossible. We know that *all things are possible* for him who believes in Christ (Mark 9:23).

I asked a mature Christian woman how I could know if the voice inside of me was from God or if it was from Satan (sometimes it can be confusing!) and she gave me some sound Biblical advice. She said anything that you hear yourself say that is condemnation is not from God. Conviction, a loving, gentle nudge that leads you into the right direction, comes from God, but God will never allow you to put yourself down. It's not in His character.

Romans 8:1-2 says *"Therefore, there is now no condemnation for those who are in Christ Jesus, because through Christ Jesus the law of the Spirit of life set me free from the law of sin and death."* So it's obvious that God does not want us to feel condemned.

I used to not be able to take a compliment very well. If someone would say "You look so nice today" I'd say "Yeah, whatever. It must be these black pants, they hide my saddlebags better than the brown ones, and my hair is just having a good day, usually it's a rats nest" (or something to that effect). It made me cringe to hear people say nice things about me because I didn't feel worthy. It's a lot different these days, though.

Now when people say something nice about me, I say "Thank you" and then I continue by giving God the glory! I'll say something like "Thank you, I appreciate that. You know, God has really blessed me". It's a lot easier for me to take a compliment when I don't feel responsible for the gifts or for the worthiness – it all comes from Christ now. It's such a free feeling.

Our pastor gave us a challenge once, and I am going to challenge you with the same activity. Every morning when you wake up, I want you to look into the mirror at yourself and say "You are a child of the King! You are a royal priesthood! You are worthy because He made you worthy!" Not only do I want you to say it, but I want you to *mean it.*

Begin praising God instead of putting yourself down. **Praise is the door to joy**. It opens the floodgates of blessing and *it blesses God, too.* How can you feel bad about yourself when you're focused on praising God? His heart must feel like bursting with joy when He sees His children praising Him. Here's an example of a prayer you can say when you're feeling down on yourself:

> *Dear Father in Heaven,*
> *Lord, I bless you. I thank you for making me just the way I am and for giving me the gift of salvation. Lord, your love is all I need! I pray that you will help me to see myself the way you see me, Lord. Thank you for your love, your mercy, your kindness and your Son, Jesus Christ. Lord, as I look around I see you everywhere. You cause the wind that blows the rain that falls and the sun that shines on me. Do not allow me to focus on my shadow, Lord, but show me how to focus on the Son that makes that shadow possible!*

*I love you Lord and I lift my voice to worship
you with everything in me!*

*In Jesus' Name I pray,
Amen*

Pray a prayer like that and God will hear you call on
Him, will call on you and He will be glorified.

I believe God gives us children to give us a glimpse of
the deep love He has for us. I look at my four children and
my heart wants to explode with love, and I know God's love
is even deeper than that.

When one of my children looks down on his or herself,
it grieves my heart like nothing else! When I see my children, I am blessed by them. I don't see their imperfections,
their sin or their human tendencies, all I see are gifts from
God (okay, so that's when they're sleeping!). But seriously,
**how do you think it makes God feel to hear us put
ourselves down?** To say we're not good enough? Or that we
are not attractive enough? As a mother, it completely breaks
my heart to hear my children say things like that. I know it
must pain God to hear me do the same.

If you are going to make a life change by balancing spiritual, mental, emotional and physical fitness, you must
begin here with your confidence. God confidence or self
confidence – which will you choose? **God is worthy** – if we
choose to put our confidence in ourselves, we will be disappointed.

CHAPTER TEN

BALANCE? WHAT'S THAT?!

I actually had finished the book, or so I thought, but the Holy Spirit confirmed to me every day for the past few weeks that there is one more chapter that needs to be addressed. Even though I don't feel very qualified to write on balance, because I'm the queen of being out of balance and have no clue how to actually achieve it, the Lord asked me to write about it.

I read Proverbs 31 and decided at that instant that I was the worst wife and mother *ever* and that I needed to figure out a way to be more "balanced" so I could be more like her. She is the Queen of Balance. If you've never read this book in Proverbs, I highly suggest you read it, but I also suggest that you keep things in perspective when you do.

You see, this beautiful, incredibly patient, gifted, organized, smart, efficient, godly and seemingly *perfect* picture of a woman which is exactly that – a picture of a woman. Not a real life, living, breathing, human woman – especially in today's world. It's good to have that nice picture to strive to achieve, but we also need to keep things a little more real.

For giggles, I'm going to do some comparisons of the portrayal of this picturesque woman with my life so we can take a reality check. (I've taken the verses from the Message format of the Bible)

- *"Her husband trusts her without reserve, and never has reason to regret it"*. **Leslie's Life:** "Her husband trusts her without reserve when it comes to anything but details, otherwise he would live to regret it".
- *"She shops around for the best yarns and cottons, and enjoys knitting and sewing."* **Leslie's Life:** "She shops for good deals and when she finds them, she purchases them even if they are not needed. She knows not how to knit and detests the details of sewing".
- *"She's up before dawn, preparing breakfast for her family and organizing her day."* **Leslie's Life:** She's up at the same time as everyone else, which is usually late. She prepares bowls of cereal for everyone and even gives them milk with it, when it is available. Her husband buys her many organizational items to try to get her to organize her life, but she has yet to use any of them for more than a week.
- *"She's skilled in the crafts of home and hearth, diligent in homemaking."* **Leslie's Life:** She's not very skilled at crafts of home and hearth, and doesn't really even know what hearth means. Her homemaking skills are anything but diligent, but she will occasionally actually find the bottom of the hamper.
- *"She makes her own clothing, and dresses in colorful linens and silks"*. **Leslie's Life:** She buys her own clothing and dresses in black most of the time because someone once told her it made her look thin. Silk is not an option, as it would require hand washing, something this woman tries to avoid.
- *"When she speaks she has something worthwhile to say, and she always says it kindly."* **Leslie's Life:**

When she speaks, she usually does so before thinking and then spends the rest of the day trying to help everyone feel better because whatever she said was taken the wrong way. She says things kindly, but not always appropriately.

• *"She keeps an eye on everyone in her household, and keeps them all busy and productive".* **Leslie's Life:** If she kept an eye on everyone in her household constantly, she'd need 6 eyes and would look like a freak. With four children, her ability to keep everyone busy and productive is limited and she realized a long time ago that kids don't usually want to sit still and read a book for a very long time.

I believe you get the picture here. *Get Real!* While reading this beautiful passage, it's important that we ask God to show us the parts about the passage that we can actually achieve through Christ, and thank Him for the attributes that we actually have. Everyone is good at something! Unrealistic expectations we put on ourselves are usually the reason we feel out of balance. Loving God with all of our heart, soul, body and mind is really all we need to be focused on. Here's what Jesus had to say about life:

*Luke 10:25-26 "On one occasion an expert in the law stood up to test Jesus. "Teacher" he asked, "what must I do to inherit eternal life?" "What is written in the Law?" he replied. "How do you read it?" He answered "Love the Lord your God with all your **heart** and with all your **soul** and with all your **strength** and with all your **mind** and love your neighbor as yourself". "You have answered correctly" Jesus replied "Do this and you will live".*

Balance is such a buzz word these days. I hear it everywhere – we need to balance work and family, balance our diets, balance our friendships, balance our tires, etc... and quite frankly, it's starting to annoy me. The reason I say that is because there is no such thing as actually achieving balance.

I prefer the word alignment. You see, when things are in alignment, you can go the distance. In order to balance something, you must stand still or at the most proceed slowly, with caution. That doesn't get you *anywhere!* I think of balance as the dangling carrot in front of the mule that keeps it going, no matter what – the mule goes for it, but never quite achieves it. Does this impede the mule's productivity? Nope. It's important we all *strive* for it, but that we don't get down on ourselves when we don't actually *achieve* it.

Our lives are full of distraction, and as a modern day woman, I know that we oftentimes put ourselves last on the importance list. So many people are deceived into thinking they must do everything for everyone – except themselves. I know I'm guilty of this occasionally. I even remember hearing the acrostic "J.O.Y." (Jesus first, others second, yourself last). I must admit, I think that's a beautiful picture, but we need to remember that putting Jesus first means you must make time in your day to spend with Him, getting to know Him better. This means taking time for your self, which is actually taking time for God.

Jesus often retreated when He was in need of rest, rejuvenation and prayer. When His ministry seemed to be drawing huge crowds, He climbed on hillsides, mountains or went to gardens to spend time alone with God or to teach to His disciples. What a wonderful example for us to follow! Even Jesus knew when He had enough. It can be downright difficult to be surrounded by people all of the time, with people wanting and needing your services, ministry or attention.

I suppose you could say Jesus was a "celebrity" of that

day. Think of the celebrities in our day – they don't get a moment alone without paparazzi taking photos, people wanting autographs, people stopping to talk, pointing, following and even stalking. Then, when they ask for peace and quiet, people almost feel as though these celebrities are not allowed to do this and they take it personally. People feel they are being cheated or "blown off" when celebrities retreat from public eye. If Jesus were walking the earth as a human today, He would make time, no matter what anyone else thought, to spend time alone with God and without people surrounding Him constantly.

If Jesus could make time for Himself, why is it that we have such a hard time doing this? **Nothing and I mean *nothing* is more important than spending time with God in prayer, reading His Word and getting to know Him personally.** If your busy life is getting in the way of this – it's time to reprioritize and refocus your attention on the true source of Joy.

Joy comes from knowing Jesus, and then sharing that joy with others. We need to quit feeling like we're being selfish when we need time for ourselves to spend with Jesus, or to rest and rejuvenate. *How much good can we do for others when we can't even take care of ourselves?*

Remember Matthew 6:33 says *"But seek first his kingdom and his righteousness, and all these things will be added unto you"*. What does "all these things" mean? It means *abundant life.*

Finding balance is a joke – striving for it is wonderful. So don't be so hard on yourself. Give yourself a break and try to remember that when we are seeking God's Kingdom first, everything else falls into alignment. We were created to love God, to love others and to show others God's love, not to be perfect and in complete balance.

PART TWO:

PHYSICAL FITNESS

CHAPTER ELEVEN

WORKING IT OFF: CARDIOVASCULAR FITNESS

B efore I begin the next few chapters on physical exercise and nutrition, I must say that it is imperative that you consult your personal physician before beginning an exercise program. It is even more important that you consult your physician if you have a pre-existing medical condition, injury or illness. Also, if this is your first time exercising, I would recommend a full-body check up. Once that is done, it's time to get moving!

A completely aligned physical fitness program should include these five components in order to be correct and effective:

1. Cardiovascular Exercise
2. Strength Training/Weight Workouts
3. Flexibility/Relaxation
4. Nutrition
5. Body Fat Composition Regulation

I'd like to begin with a chapter on cardiovascular exercise.

I will be going over the basics, in language you can understand so you can get a firm grip on what cardiovascular, or "aerobic" activity is and what it can do for you.

I absolutely love aerobics. I've been doing aerobics for over 11 years now and I can tell you, it's a lot of fun for me. But I remember when I first started, I hated it. I remember just feeling completely exhausted and wondering if it would ever get easier or enjoyable. Well, it did. It just took patience and time to help me get to a place where I actually enjoy it.

Aerobics classes are great – but there is more to cardiovascular exercise than just going to an organized aerobics class. Cardiovascular exercise is basically just anything that gets your heart rate up and warms your core body temperature.

I have heard so many people say "I just don't like to sweat" or "nothing interests me". I decided to put together a list that shows all the different things you can possibly do that can raise your heart rate. Here's what I came up with:

A – Athletic Conditioning
B – Boxing
C- Cycling
D – Double Step Aerobics
E – Electric Slide
F – Funk Aerobics
G – Go-Go-Dancing
H – Hip Hop Dancing
I – Interval Training
J – Jump Rope
K – Kickboxing
L – Low Impact Aerobics
M – Marathon Running
N – Nature Hiking
O – Oar Rowing (kayaking, canoeing)

P – Pilates
Q – Quick Sprints
R – Roller Blading
S – Swimming
T – Tennis
U – Underwater Aerobics
V – Vertical Step Classes
W – Walking
X – X-treme Sports (for the daring!)
Y – Yoga (Christ-centered, not self-centered)
Z – Zumba®

I'm sure from the list above there is something that might interest you. It's important that we find or make time for cardiovascular exercise. Here are some of the important benefits of including aerobic activity into your exercise routine:
- Increases endurance
- Increases life expectancy
- Burns considerable amounts of fat
- Increases metabolism
- Improves energy
- Improves lung function
- Lowers blood pressure
- Helps circulation
- Lifts up your mood
- Improves range of motion

If you are currently not exercising, just look over the benefits it offers to you and consider adding it into your schedule. Really, all you need to do to get started is commit to 30 minutes, 3 times per week. Get yourself into a routine, so that you can make a habit out of it. Don't try to pressure yourself into doing too much too soon but take time to educate yourself and develop good habits.

Exercise should be as much of your routine as brushing your teeth. I've come to a place in my life where if I don't exercise, I feel like something is missing. It can become like that for you, too. It just takes time, patience, commitment and maybe even some accountability.

Keeping your prayer life saturated with prayers that God will give you the strength, energy and desire to work out is a good place to start. He wants what's best for you.

Being spiritually fit is a good start before trying to be physically fit. They really compliment each other so well.

I am struck by how similar the disciplines of a Christian walk and fitness are. When you are studying your Bible, immersed in prayer and walking daily with the Lord, you become spiritually fit. Often, the Lord will ask you to "step out of your comfort zone" in order to keep your zeal. So it is with physical fitness – you must learn about fitness, work-out consistently and never become comfortable with your routine. Always remember that if you are comfortable and settled, it might be time to shake up your routine a bit – you want to keep yourself challenged.

When you do cardiovascular exercise, it's important to know how hard you should be working. It's important that you find out what your maximum heart rate is. The simple way to determine this is to take the number 220 and minus your age. That is the absolute top end of where your heart rate per minute should be. Once you determine this number, take 65-85% of that number to determine your "heart rate range" – the range you want to be in for a 1-minute count.

Take your pulse for 10 seconds after you have been working out for 5-10 minutes. Begin counting with zero, then count up until the 10 seconds are up. Take this number and multiply it by 6 to get your heart rate. I prefer to count for 6 seconds and then just add a zero, but I've been told this is not quite as accurate. There are many other complicated methods you can use to determine your target heart rate, but

I find this method is the most simple.

You will not have to continually take your heart rate every few minutes once you've been exercising for awhile, because you will know what your body feels like when it's in "the zone". In fitness, we often refer to the "talk test" – that means if you can talk without feeling overwhelmed or breathing too hard, you're probably in your target heart rate zone.

Sometimes, in my classes I will ask people how they feel on a scale of 1-10, 1 being "not much" and 10 being "Wow – I'm wiped out!" You might benefit from a self-test like that.

In your quest to be physically fit, please remember that moderation is the key. If you are doing too much too soon, you may experience muscle loss, forgetfulness, and burnout or overuse injuries. Remember, it is QUALITY, not QUANTITY. You will also want to vary your workouts often so your body is challenged in different ways.

There is no blanket prescription for everyone when it comes to exercise because we are all uniquely made. What works for your friend may not work for you, so do not become discouraged and give up. Just keep looking and trying things until you find the perfect fit for your lifestyle, your interests and biological make-up.

You will want to increase the frequency, the intensity and the duration of your workouts as you get "comfortable", so be very mindful of this. Thirty minutes, 3 times per week is a great way to start, but you wouldn't want to stay there forever. Challenge yourself and set small, attainable goals so you can see results.

Most of all have fun! Enjoy your workouts. I mentioned in a previous chapter that my exercise sessions are sometimes spent praying and listening to praise music. This makes my workouts not only effective spiritually, but also physically and mentally.

Once you find a cardiovascular routine that compliments

your interests and goals, then you can look into incorporating some resistance training, or weight training.

> *1 Corinthians 7:1 "Since we have these promises, dear friends, let us purify ourselves from everything that contaminates body and spirit, perfecting holiness out of reverence for God".*

CHAPTER TWELVE

WHY WEIGHTS?

If weights are a new concept to you, don't fear. I'm here to dispel myths, give you valuable information and show you how to incorporate a resistance training routine into your life that is non-intimidating and extremely beneficial.

Here are some of the benefits of incorporating weight resistance training into your life:

- Increased muscle density
- Increased bone density
- Lowered body fat
- Increased metabolism
- Improve balance and coordination
- Increased strength and endurance
- Higher confidence level
- Improved posture
- Improved muscular appearance and tone
- Improved efficiency in performing daily activities

Those are certainly a lot of great benefits. I noticed that it doesn't say "improved hulk-like appearance" up there anywhere. Actually, weights will help make you more look compact, not bulk you up. Men tend to bulk up a little more due to their testosterone levels and ability to lift heavier weight, but women just get more compact under normal conditions.

Let me address you ladies here for a minute. A lot of women are fearful of strength training because they have seen the women on the television or magazines who enter the body building competitions and they are terrified if they lift weights they will look that way.

Please let me dispel that myth. Women who compete in body building competitions are usually training an awful lot with a tremendous workload. Their diets are very, very strict and they actually become almost dehydrated right before the competition to make their muscles stand out more. Some (but not all) are also taking supplements that increase their muscle mass. You *will not* get a body like that with regular strength training or conditioning and you *can not* get a body like that with a normal, healthy, balanced diet.

People who lift weights are more defined, more toned, have better posture and have a healthy appearance. We are born with a certain amount of attainable muscle, and no matter what, our muscles will not grow beyond our genetic capabilities, even with training.

I have heard women say they are afraid they are going to "push the fat" out further by building muscle. Not true. You see, when you increase muscle density through training, you are increasing your metabolism, which in turn, will actually burn the fat that lies on top of the muscle. It is a very, very effective way to change the shape of your body.

I'm going to explain, in very simple terms, how the body works when it comes to weight training. You see, the muscle is actually going through a "tearing down" phase when you are in the process of working out. Your body must accommodate this by rebuilding (or repairing) the muscle once the damage is done.

This process takes a tremendous amount of energy and

time. In order to get the energy your muscles need in order to rebuild, your metabolism will increase. Think of it this way: your muscles are like furnaces in your body. The more you work them by heating them up (or working them out), the hotter they get. What happens to fat when it gets hot? It melts. Building muscle, in a way, melts fat from your body. OK, so where does the fat go, you might ask. It goes toward the energy your body needs to rebuild and repair the muscle.

Once the muscle is repaired, it becomes stronger and more efficient. Because of this rebuilding process, you must have adequate rest between weighted work outs of the same muscle group. For instance, if you work out your chest, it's important you wait about 48 hours to allow the muscle to completely repair before stressing it again.

You know, it's funny - only in weight training do the words "failure", "fatigue", "tear-down" and "stress" actually mean something good! When you are weight training, you want to be able to really "stress" the muscle to the point of "tearing it down", which is usually the point of either "fatigue" (when your muscle is almost at that point of total exhaustion, but not quite) or "failure" (you cannot possibly do one more repetition).

Only once you've reached that point does your body respond by rebuilding. The body is amazingly adaptable. The more you train, the more efficient your muscles become! Being in the fitness field, I am always amazed by how God created such intricate, efficient bodies for us to live in.

Now that you understand how weight training works and how your body responds to it, let me give you some guidelines on how to introduce weights into your routine. First, let me highly suggest even just one session with a professional personal trainer, who can show you specifically how to lift the weights without injuring yourself and they can help you set short term goals. If you do not want to do this, don't worry – you can still get a good workout, it will just take a lot of the guesswork out of the routine if you have someone there with you who is professionally trained.

Here are some generalized guidelines:

- When lifting, you should really start feeling a lot of resistance on about the 8th repetition. If you do not, you are probably not challenging yourself enough. I would go no more than 16 repetitions, and if you are just starting out, 10-12 is probably plenty.
- Beginners should start with 1 full set of repetitions. Once you are comfortable with this routine, add another set. Continue listening to your body and making necessary adjustments in the amount of weight lifted, the amount of repetitions and the number of sets.
- Lift 3 times per week for optimum results, with 48 hours of rest between each resistance workout for the same muscle group.
- Never lock out your joints (stiffen and hyperextend) when lifting. This can injure or impair your joint and cause injury, pain and inflammation.
- Try to go slow and controlled, breathing in on the contraction (shortening of the muscle) and breathing out on the extension (lengthening of the muscle). Breathing is very important – it keeps oxygen going to the cells and helps control the amount of lactic acid build up in the muscle. It also helps keep you focused.
- Start with the larger muscle groups first. For a full upper body workout, you would want to go in this order: chest, back, shoulders, tricep, bicep. For a full lower body workout, you want to go in this order: hamstrings, quadriceps, glutes (bottom), outer thigh, inner thigh, calves. The reason you start with the larger groups first is because you gain the most

strength from these groups and when you lift with the smaller groups, the larger ones play an important role in assisting with those movements, so you don't want to wear out the larger ones before you get to isolate them.

- Keep a journal of each work out. Jot down the exercise, the weight, the number of sets and any adjustments you had to make during the exercise.
- Stretch the muscles after you work them to help break up the lactic acid, improve flexibility and reduce delayed onset soreness.
- Be creative with what you lift – don't always do the same exercises for the same muscle groups. You want to challenge your body in different ways and you don't want to get bored or lazy with the workload.
- Keep your abdominals contracted throughout your workout. Imagine you have on a girdle and someone is tightening it when you lift the weight. This helps you stay balanced, focused and it actually improves your performance. It also gives you a great abdominal toning workout.
- Abdominal work can be inserted anywhere in your routine, but most people save the best for last. It's up to you – it doesn't matter where you fit it in as long as you do it at some point. The "core" or trunk of your body is extremely important in balance, agility and posture, so keep it strong.
- If it hurts, STOP.

These pointers should help you get started. Don't let the gym or the weights intimidate you – they are not difficult to learn about at all. It's an important gift you can give yourself, so don't let your pride or fear get in the way.

Please remember that when you are strength training,

your weight on a scale may increase. I highly recommend you throw out your scale! Muscle is denser than fat and a pound of muscle takes up 1/3 of the amount of space as a pound of fat, though it might weigh more. So keep things in perspective. I'd have a doctor or trainer read your body fat measurement and you can go by that number if you are a numbers person. If you're not, just go by how you feel and how your clothes fit. It's hard for some of us to get past the whole scale thing but it's important that you understand that weight is subjective.

I want to touch on the importance of flexibility training for a moment. While teaching my group fitness classes, I notice that at the end, when we are cooling down and stretching, a lot of people end up leaving. It's so important that you stretch your body after you work out. Stick around for the cool down in a group fitness class and make sure that if you are working out on your own that you take time to stretch afterward.

You see, your body works very hard during physical exercise. When we work, we expect to get paid, right? So it is with our muscles – and this is how we pay them: we stretch them and give them the thanks and reward they deserve for a job well done. When we stretch, we are helping to break up the lactic acid that gets stored in the muscle during exertion, and this can help alleviate soreness and stiffness. It also helps increase your flexibility, which in turn will give you better range of motion, lessen your chances of injury and give you longer, leaner muscles.

It's always a good time to stretch at the end of the workout, because your body is warmed up and ready. Think about taffy for a moment. When it is cold, it is stiff, not pliable and if you try to stretch it, it breaks. However, when it's warm, it is pliable, easy to maneuver and a lot less likely to break. That's how it is with your muscles. Stretching when warm is a wonderful way to increase flexibility.

Stretching at the beginning of a workout should be done in a rhythmic way (short hold stretches that increase blood flow and prepare muscles for movement, but not flexibility).

You only get one shot at keeping your temple in shape for God's work. How are you going to spend the time you have here in your body? If you are living a sedentary, unfruitful life, it's never too late to change. Ask God to help you find the body you were created to have and then get moving!

> *1 Corinthians 9:25 "Everyone who competes in the games goes into strict training. They do it to get a crown that will not last; but we do it to get a crown that will last forever."*

CHAPTER THIRTEEN

FOOD FOR THOUGHT (NUTRITION'S PREPARED BALANCE APPROACH)

I always encourage my clients to think of food as a fuel for their body, instead of thinking of it as a reward or even as an enemy. Yes, we enjoy food and I'm sure God created taste buds so we could savor the different flavors out there, so I'm not saying that food is bad – but I'm saying we cannot make it our god of choice. We all need food to survive, but too little of it or too much of it can be devastating to your system.

I realize there are many fad diets out there that claim to have the perfect plan for your body to lose weight. I get so frustrated seeing some of these diets. We are all unique individuals who metabolize differently, have different appetites, crave different foods and live in different cultures. There is no one diet that can work for every body.

There's a running joke in the nutrition and fitness industry that says "What do all diets have in common: Failure!". That's because once you tell yourself you're going to go on a diet, you immediately start thinking about what you're going to eat next. Many of these diets omit your favorite foods, so in your deprivation mode, you crave them even more. You might be able to succeed in the diet for awhile, but when you start eating a normal diet again, you will probably gain the weight, and then some, back because you are eating those same foods again. Wouldn't it be a better idea to change your lifestyle?

Rather than denying yourself your favorite foods, try living your life in moderation. I know many nutritionists recommend you only eat when you are hungry, but I must disagree with that notion. If you only eat when you are hungry, you are using food to curb hunger, instead of fuel your body and you will be more likely to make a poor food choice due to the effects that feeling hungry have on your ability to make wise choices.

When we look at food as a fuel, we realize that if we are proactive in our eating, instead of reactive, we make better choices and we eat less.

I recommend that you try the Prepared Balance Approach, and make it a lifestyle. The way you do this is simple: You prepare ahead and then balance your meals. The meals should be every 3-4 hours and should be smaller in portion. You should be eating 5-6 meals per day. You will be eating before you get overly hungry, so your overeating tendency will not be as fierce.

Your meals should consist of a palm or fist sized (your palm, not someone with bigger hands!) portion of protein and a palm sized portion of a complex carbohydrate (starch) and all the green, leafy veggies you want. An example of a day's worth of eating would be:

6am – yogurt (this has protein and carbohydrates – already
      balanced, but be aware of the sugar content)
9am – boiled egg & 1 piece of wheat toast

12pm – tuna on 1 piece of wheat toast with a leafy, green salad

3pm – protein bar (there are many tasty varieties on the market that have a combination of protein & carbohydrates!)

6pm – chicken breast, brown rice, broccoli

9pm – apple with peanut butter

These are things that can set you up for failure in a "diet":

- Eating foods you hate
- Excluding a certain food group
- Having to measure food before you eat it (too much work!)
- Having to count calories
- Allowing yourself to get too hungry
- Feeding your family something different than what you are eating
- Lack of preparation
- Giving up too soon

Let's discuss preparation. In my family, we like to use Sunday afternoons for the preparation phase of our week. We make a menu for the week, shop accordingly and when I return, I grill chicken breasts, low-fat hamburger patties, and lean cuts of beef. I also boil some eggs. When the grilling and boiling is done, I store the already prepared meat in individual zipper bags in the freezer and the hard-boiled eggs in a large gallon-size zipper bag (or they will smell up your refrigerator!). As we need a quick protein during the week, we can grab an individual meat portion from the freezer and microwave it for 90 seconds for a meal.

I've found that complex carbohydrates are fairly easy to get and they don't require much preparation. These would include fruits, starchy vegetables, whole wheat grains and cereals and legumes. You might want to boil some brown rice and store it in individual containers or prepare some pasta ahead of time, but for the most part, the protein is what needs to be prepared ahead of time. That's why so many of us are carbohydrate addicts – they are easy, fast and readily available – especially the simple carbohydrates (sugary, sweet stuff). So as you can see, preparation can be vital in the success of your new lifestyle!

Carbohydrates have gotten a very bad rap lately with all the low or no-carbohydrate diets out there. Actually, a diet with comparable calories that is higher in fat is going to sabotage your efforts more so than a diet with the same amount of calories that are coming from complex carbohydrates. Starchy foods are a great source of energy for people who are trying to lose weight.

The key to eating carbohydrates is to remember the portion control. Look at your palm, then place your other fist on top of it. That's about the size of 1 portion of food, no matter if it's protein, carbohydrate or vegetable. That's the simplest way I can describe it. When we start weighing foods, or talking in ounces or grams or counting calories I find I lose people quite frequently. I always say the simpler, the better.

Complex carbohydrates can contain high amounts of the important nutrient, fiber. Fiber is essential in the digestion process. Fiber gives your body the necessary "push" it needs to push the food through the digestion process. It reduces the symptoms of chronic constipation, diverticular disease and some types of irritable bowel syndrome. According to the Dietary Guidelines for Americans, from the US Department of Agriculture and health, "It has been suggested that diets low in fiber may increase the risk of developing colon cancer". This is important news – and it should be an important consideration for you as you begin your new lifestyle.

Proteins are especially important, too, and should make up about 30% of your total calories daily. If you control the portions (by using the fist in palm method) you should stay within that range. Foods higher in protein will help you feel satisfied longer, will give your body something to digest for awhile (it takes longer to digest than carbohydrates) so it will temporarily increase your metabolism after eating it, and they also help release stored carbohydrates from the liver. Lack of protein in your diet can contribute to:

- Slowed immune system
- Inhibited growth potential (height)
- Reduced longevity
- Inhibited muscle growth/density
- Fatigue and weakness
- Eventual weight gain
- Accelerated aging

Some sources of protein include chicken, fish, beef, low fat cottage cheese, nuts, peanut butter, low fat milk, soy, eggs/egg whites, whey, beans, and pork, supplements (protein shakes and nutrition bars).

It might surprise you that studies have been done that support the fact that drinking water can actually reduce fat deposits in your body. When we don't drink enough water, it puts stress on our bodies because the kidneys cannot function properly without it. When that happens, a majority of the kidney's workload is placed on the liver, which is usually supposed to be metabolizing stored fat for energy. When it's distracted by doing the job of the kidneys, fat metabolizing is hindered. So it would make sense that if you drink water, your kidneys are able to function properly, allowing the liver to do its assigned job of metabolizing fat. *God made our bodies a lot smarter than we could ever imagine, didn't He?*

You should be drinking at the very least 8 glasses of water per day. If you work out, you should increase this even more. When we lose a dramatic amount of weight, sometimes we are left with "sagging skin" on our bodies. If you are drinking enough water, you can help reduce this effect because drinking water helps maintain muscle tone and can keep your cells supple and well-nourished during the weight-loss process. Your body will function best when it is hydrated, so give yourself the gift of drinking plenty of cell-nourishing, thirst-quenching water.

I must address the importance of not starving yourself in order to lose weight. You see, when you don't eat, your body (which God made extremely smart) thinks you are going into starvation mode. As a result, it slows down your metabolism dramatically. It stores food it would normally use for fuel as fat, just in case you need reserves should the situation get worse. *So it's extremely counterproductive, not to mention extremely dangerous, to starve yourself to lose weight.*

People who try losing weight this way usually end up extremely tired, weak and their blood sugar levels plummet. In anorexia nervosa, the body is so desperate for fuel that it starts eating away at the internal organs, sort of feeding on itself. Many people with this eating disorder, if they survive, walk away with organ damage. It does not make sense to do this to yourself – remember, you are God's holy temple. If you feel you are in a dangerous direction, going toward this eating disorder, you must seek out professional help immediately. You can beat it – with lots of patience, prayer and professional help.

So what we need to remember is that food is not a friend, a foe or a fulfiller – but it is a fuel that your body needs in order to function. *Moderation is the key, portion control is essential and preparation can make your life a lot easier.* It's much easier to make a lifestyle change like this when you have enlisted the support of your family, so get them involved in the planning and preparations so you can live healthy, once and for all.

John 6:48-51 (Jesus said) "I am the bread of life. Your forefathers ate the manna in the desert, yet they died. But here is the bread that comes down from heaven, which a man may eat and not die. I am the living bread that came down from heaven. If anyone eats of this bread, he will live forever. This bread is my flesh, which I will give for the life of the world."

PART THREE:

ETERNAL FITNESS

CHAPTER FOURTEEN

DEAR DIARY

The importance of keeping a journal can only be described as "of utmost" in the whole effectiveness of spiritual, mental and physical fitness success. The entries do not need to be lengthy, they do not need to be in perfect writing, and they don't even need to be hand written. A lot of people type their entries on their computers and store them in a file specified as "journal". Personally, I find a written entry is easier and is something I can do while lying in bed before I go to sleep, but no matter how you prefer to do it, *just do it!*

I use my journal for many things, including:

- Keeping record of my food consumption during the day
- Keeping record of my exercise for the day
- Prayer requests
- Exciting events that happen that show God at work in my life
- Setting goals
- Writing down important thoughts as they come to me

There really is no rule written about what you should

include, but let me offer up a few suggestions for you. If this is new to you, don't put pressure on yourself to do it perfectly every day. Enter just the food and exercise for awhile. If you are in the process of losing weight, you might even want to jot down your measurements and take them every 6-8 weeks or so, so you can see your progress.

As you get more comfortable with the journal, start writing prayer requests. I sometimes even write my prayers down, so I can go back and say them again and again. I like to do this because when I look back over the diary months later or even years later, I see that God was faithful in everything. I can't describe the excitement I experience when that happens! It's such a beautiful gift.

When I set goals for myself, I find myself more accountable when I write them down. The Bible is a perfect model of the accountability in writing things down. When the Holy Spirit communicates to you that you should write something, you should do it. Look at this verse, for example:

- **Isaiah 30:8** *Go now, write it on a tablet for them, and inscribe it on a scroll, that for the days to come it may be an everlasting witness.*

Writing makes us accountable to ourselves, to our families and especially to God. Isaiah understood that and look what happened when he wrote things down! Our words will never even come close to the awesomeness of God's word, but the model of writing things down is beautiful.

Even when Job was going through the difficult times he faced, he wanted nothing more than his words to be recorded so people could see God's faithfulness. Take a look at this verse from the book of Job: **Job 19:23** *"Oh, that my words were recorded, that they were written on a scroll"*. I suppose you see the importance now. So let's get started on your first entry!

First, record your goals for the next year for yourself, spiritually, physically and mentally. What will you do to improve your lifestyle this year? Are you going to be more faithful in your Bible study? How about your exercise routine (if you even have one yet)? Think about it, pray and allow God to show you what He wants for you this year. Once you have the thoughts together, date the page and write the goals down.

Now that your goals are written, you are accountable to them. I want you to stop right now, get out some stationary or whatever paper you can gather. Also, find an envelope you can seal and put it aside. Now, write yourself a letter. Here's what you could include in this letter to yourself:

- Thank yourself for making positive life changes during the next year
- Write down those goals you just set for yourself in the letter
- Write down the reasons why you made those positive life changes (to feel better, to be more productive, because God wants you to, for your children or spouse, because you want to live to see you great-grandchildren's wedding, etc…)
- Date the letter with today's date
- Fold it and put it in the envelope and seal it. Write on the envelope "To (insert your name), open on (insert today's date, but date it with the next year).

Now you've already succeeded in your eyes, right? No fear of failure here. You know it's been done, and you're already going to thank yourself for the efforts you are going to put forth this year. What a concept. You wrote down the goal, already accepted it as truth and put your faith in the fact that it would come to pass. Now you can live daily without fear of failing, because it's already been done! Remember, God doesn't give us a spirit of fear, but a spirit of power, love and self-discipline (2 Timothy 1:7).

Now that you've written your letter, put it in the envelope, date it, put it aside and just pray about what God wants you to include in your journal entry every day. He will show you what you need to write, and the more you drench yourself in the promises in His word, the more you will see clearly what His plan for your life is. Living in God's will is the most amazingly rewarding place to be!

Once you've completed your letter to yourself, take another piece of paper and jot down some scripture references that encourage, challenge and motivate you in your new life change. Give the goals to God, asking for His provisions along the way. He wants you to come to Him and give everything to Him. Keep these scriptures in your journal for quick reference. Memorization is essential, too, as quoting scripture when confronted with temptation or a stronghold is a mighty weapon, a sword of the Spirit (Ephesians 6:17).

You might want to have 2 journals – one for food & exercise (physical fitness) and one for prayer, praises & goals (spiritual fitness). Whatever you decide to do, I would like to hear from you in a year. I want to know the journey you've been on and how your life has changed. It blesses me to share this information with you and I pray it will bless you, too. What a joy it would be to hear from you in a year, after you open your letter, and hear about how God worked in your life.

Many, many blessings to all of you as you begin your journey of building the body of Christ (your body) through complete fitness.

APPENDIX A:

ETERNAL FITNESS

A lot of people, especially in America, say they are Christians. There is a lot of confusion about what it means to be a Christian. God's Word clearly spells out this wonderful plan for you, but people assume that if they are good, never kill anyone, go to church and do good deeds, then that makes them a Christian. This is a lie that Satan wants to saturate our society with because it gives a false sense of security.

God is perfect and holy and it is not in His character to sin. He hates sin. When man sinned, He was devastated and sickened. Throughout the Old Testament, we read about how people offered up sacrifices for their sin so they could be acceptable to God. Also, throughout the Old Testament (especially in the books of Isaiah and Micah), we are told of the coming "Messiah" (the expected king and deliver of the Jews) who would be the ultimate sacrifice for sin.

There were hundreds of prophecies in the Old Testament that predicted this Messiah. People didn't know who or when, but they had many signs revealed through prophets whom God appointed to speak through. Jesus Christ fulfilled each and every prophecy given in the Old Testament. He is that promised Messiah! God sent His son down to the earth so He could become the sacrifice for our sin.

This is a free gift from God, available for all. John 3:16 says *"For God so loved the world that He gave His only begotten son, that whosoever believes in Him shall not perish, but have everlasting life"*. This salvation is available to all, but unfortunately, not all will accept this free gift. Yes, it is free, but in a way, it will cost you your life. You must make Jesus Lord of everything you say and do, so He can live through you. Some people, rather it be from pride, selfishness or ignorance, will not accept Christ. Jesus knew this would happen.

Jesus said in Matthew 7:13 *"Enter through the narrow gate. For wide is the gate and broad is the road that leads to destruction, and many enter through it. But small is the gate and narrow the road that leads to life and only a few find it"*.

This is a sad verse, in my opinion. My resistance to God came from the fact that I cared more about what others thought about me than what God did. I wanted to "fit in" and be accepted and I knew that Christians seemed "different". Paul said it best:

- *"It seems to me that God has put us (Christians) who bear his Message on stage in a theater in which no one wants to buy a ticket. We're something everyone stands around and stares at, like an accident in the street. We're the Messiah's Misfits...you might be well-thought-of by others, but we're mostly kicked around...we get doors slammed in our faces....when they call us names, we say "God bless you". When they spread rumors about us, we put in a good word for them. We're treated like garbage, potato peelings from the culture's kitchen."*
  - *1 Corinthians 4 (The Message)*

Paul makes me laugh sometimes, but he's right. The

world sees Christians this way. Jesus warned us that this would happen. He said in John 15:18-19 *"If the world hates you, keep in mind that it hated me first. If you belonged to the world, it would love you as its own. As it is, you do not belong to the world, but I have chosen you out of the world. That is why the world hates you."* What a comfort to realize that Jesus suffered persecution beyond what we could imagine, so He understands how we feel better than anyone.

When you surround yourself with God and other believers, you will experience more love than you could ever imagine. I was so caught up in being liked by the world, that what I had to do was understand that what people think of me is temporary. We are only here in the world for a little while, but our souls go on for eternity. My ambition is to please God, not man now. I am not saying it's easy, but it's eternally worth it and the joy you feel when God is pleased far outweighs the happiness you feel when the world is. Happiness is temporary and doesn't penetrate the soul like joy does!

To know, without a doubt, that you are a Christian is the most incredible blessing you will ever receive. God wants to bless you! If you have never accepted Christ as your savior, I urge you to seek His face, confess your sin, repent and turn away from your sin accept His offering for your sin and make Jesus Christ the Lord of your life.

The following prayer, when said from the heart with true repentance (not just saying "I'm sorry" but saying "I'm through with sin!"), will bring you into a relationship with Christ and your life will never be the same again – it will be abundant and purposeful! Please, if you have never said this prayer and believed it with the full surrender of self, repeat it right now:

Dear Heavenly Father,
I confess that I am a sinner and I need your forgiveness. I do not want to be controlled by sin anymore, but I want to follow righteousness through your son, Jesus Christ! Jesus, thank you for dying on the cross for my sin. I repent of my sin and ask that you be the Lord and Savior of my life. I know that you are the way, the truth and the life and I want to walk the rest of my life with you, Lord. Please guide me to truth, lead me into understanding and give me wisdom as I study the Bible and walk the Christian walk with you by my side. Thank you for your forgiveness, your mercy and your grace! In Jesus' name I pray, Amen.

If you just prayed that prayer from your heart, you are going to spend eternity with Jesus Christ! Now, God's Word says that you should get into a Bible based church and grow spiritually. Surround yourself with Christian friends, continue to pray and read your Bible every day. God speaks to us through His word – it's a precious gift. Don't neglect your faith – it's the most important relationship you have.

I'd love to share your joy with you – please e-mail me at lnease@potentialunlimited.us and share with me about your decision to follow Christ so I can pray for you and rejoice! God is good!

John 15:4&5 "Remain in me and I will remain in you...apart from me, you can do nothing".

PERSONAL REFLECTION & GROUP DISCUSSION QUESTIONS

APPENDIX B:

PERSONAL REFLECTION AND GROUP DISCUSSION QUESTIONS

If you would like to use this book in a group study, or if you want to take some personal reflection and application, here are some questions for you that may encourage discussion or give guidance on how you can apply the Biblical truths in Body Builders to your life.

CHAPTER ONE: OUT OF THE DARKNESS & INTO THE LIGHT (MY STORY)

Personal Reflection: Write your testimony out (or type it) and reflect on God's goodness and faithfulness in your life. Share your testimony this week and see how God can use your story to reach out to others who are in need of spiritual fitness. If this exercise is difficult for you, seek out someone who you respect, spiritually. They would be glad to help you because God has called us to help one another.

Group Study: Each of you write out your testimony and share it with the group. Discuss how your life experiences have shaped you into the person you are today and how you can use your story to help others.

CHAPTER TWO: GOD'S HOLY TEMPLE
1. How are you treating God's Temple? Is there room for improvement? If so, what steps are you going to take to change?
2. Did the Holy Spirit speak to you about something specific during the reading of this chapter? If so, what did He say?

CHAPTER THREE: FAT AND HAPPY IN AMERICA
1. Has food ever been a master to you? When and why do you eat?
2. Before you found Christ, what were you using to build your "tower of Babel" to God?
3. Now that you have found Christ, what does Satan use to distract you from Him?

CHAPTER FOUR: WHY ARE WE SO SILENT?
1. Why do you think gluttony is such a silent epidemic among Christians?
2. Now that you are a new creation in Christ, how are you going to remain focused on Him?
3. What scriptures do you find helpful in your walk with God? Meditate on them.

CHAPTER FIVE: TRUTH OR CONSEQUENCES?
1. How do you handle constructive criticism?
2. Think of a story (and share it if you are in a group) of how constructive criticism helped you improve in an area of your life.
3. Have you ever tried to do the work of the Holy Spirit? How did it turn out?
4. Has church ever let you down? If so, why do you think this happened? Read Hebrews 10:24-25 and

share what God tells you about the church.

CHAPTER SIX: PAUSE FOR THE CAUSE
1. Has God ever taken an everyday situation and made it into a teachable moment for you? What did you glean from it?
2. Think of a problem you are faced with right now. Lay it at God's feet and give it completely to Him. As you do, step away from the situation, get into God's Word and find the answers you have not been able to find. Then, give Him the glory by sharing your story with someone. Praise the Lord for His provisions!

CHAPTER SEVEN: COMPLETE FITNESS ("CROSS TRAINING")
1. What areas in your life need some nurturing? What steps will you take to be more in alignment?
2. Do you have a dream that you have not accomplished yet? Share it with your group. Write down specific steps you will take to achieve your dream.
3. Read Acts chapter 9. Discuss what this story means to us today.
4. Begin, this week, asking yourself before making any decision "If I do this, will it lead me to a place where I can glorify God?" and make a decision based on the answer you get. See what transpires in your life as a result and share it with the group!

CHAPTER EIGHT: I'LL START ON MONDAY
1. Is there something you've been putting off (a decision, a lifestyle change, an activity)?
2. If fear of failure were not a factor, what would you do?
3. What are some steps you can take to overcome your

fears and stop procrastinating?

CHAPTER NINE: WALKING IN CONFIDENCE

1. What are some exercises you can do daily that will increase your confidence? (for example, compliment 5 people every day, accept compliments graciously, give God glory, etc..)
2. Are you gleaning your confidence from God or from others' opinions of you? Do this exercise: Put an X on the line where you fall. Then place on O on the line where you want to be:
GOD————————————————————MAN
3. Are you focusing on the eternal or the temporal? What changes do you need to make in your life?
4. If you are in a group study, give each person there a true compliment. If you are the one receiving the compliment, somehow give God the glory in your mind and accept the compliment with grace. Pass it on!

CHAPTER TEN: BALANCE? WHAT'S THAT?!

1. Women: Have you been trying to live up to the Proverbs 31 woman? If so, what have the results been?
2. Men: What unrealistic expectations have you been trying to live up to? What have the results been?
3. Have you been taking time to refuel in your life? If not, why?
4. Commit right now to making time, each day, for yourself to refuel and seek God's Will for you life.

CHAPTER ELEVEN: WORKING IT OFF (CARDIO-VASCULAR FITNESS)

1. Are you currently in an exercise program? If so, what do you do and if not, what are you going to do?

2. From the A to Z list, jot down and share some exercise ideas that suit your personality. Commit to trying at least 2 in the next week. If you have other ideas, share them with the group!
3. What is your target heart rate?

CHAPTER TWELVE: WHY WEIGHTS?

1. Have you ever been on a strength training routine? If so, what was it like? If not, why?
2. Either schedule 1 session with a personal trainer to learn to use weights, or write yourself up a routine using the information in this chapter as a guideline. Share your routine with the group and hold yourselves accountable to each other.
3. Is there a buddy you can work out with? Pray and ask God to reveal to you if there is someone He feels might also want a buddy and make it your goal to contact this person this week.

CHAPTER THIRTEEN: FOOD FOR THOUGHT

1. Write out a menu for the week and shop accordingly. Prepare snacks in advance and see what happens! Use the Prepared Balance approach and try it for a week. How did you feel? Were you energized? Did you get hungry? Was it easy or difficult for you and why? Share your experiences.
2. What do you find most difficult about changing your way of eating? What did you find most easy?

CHAPTER FOURTEEN: DEAR DIARY

1. Write the letter to yourself that was discussed in this chapter. What were some of your reasons for change? Everyone bring your letters and share them (if you are comfortable doing so). Seal them together and give them to the designated leader of

the group. Schedule a meeting in 1 year to open your letters and rejoice in your progress as a group.
2.   Start journaling TODAY!

I hope you enjoyed this journey of Complete Fitness through Body Builders. I would love to hear about your group's experiences. If you need ideas on accountability groups, how to incorporate exercise classes into your church or if you need ideas for food, fitness or how to have fun while working out, always feel free to contact me at any time. You can do this. I trust you see now that there is nothing that is impossible for those who put God first in their lives.

Romans 15:13 "May the God of hope fill you with all joy and peace as you trust in him, so that you may overflow with hope by the power of the Holy Spirit".

Printed in the United States
125006LV00003B/2/A